Traditional Stickmaking

CHARLIE WALKER

THE CROWOOD PRESS

First published in 2016 by
The Crowood Press Ltd
Ramsbury, Marlborough
Wiltshire SN8 2HR

www.crowood.com

British Library Cataloguing-in-Publication Data
A catalogue record for this book is available from the British Library.

ISBN 978 1 78500 110 9

Frontispiece: A collection of sticks made by the author.

Acknowledgements
I would like to thank all the stickmakers who have helped me over the last few
years, and especially Gordon Flintoft, who has been my mentor since I began this
absorbing hobby. I also wish to remember two very close friends, John Penny and
George Russell, who have sadly passed away; they both willingly gave me help and
advice, which was very much appreciated. Lastly my thanks to my neighbour Geoff,
who drew the two sketches used in this book.

Typeset by Jean Cussons Typesetting, Diss, Norfolk
Printed and bound in India by Replika Press Pvt Ltd

CONTENTS

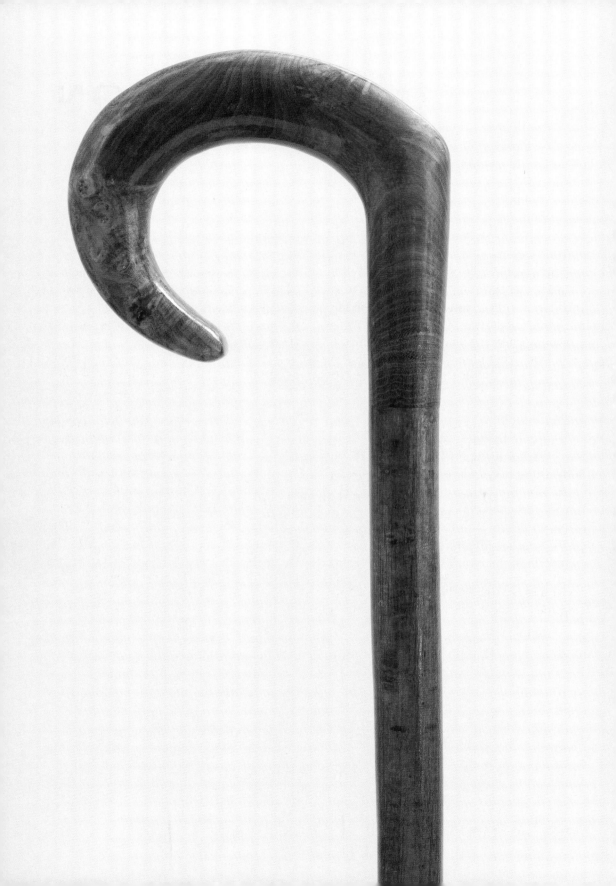

INTRODUCTION

This book is intended to help anyone wanting to make sticks for work or pleasure using tried and tested techniques with traditional materials. It provides advice on some of the tools and equipment needed to make a variety of sticks and handles out of materials including wood, antler, buffalo and sheep horn, and concludes with a feature on decorating handles. It includes suggestions on methods of storing, straightening and jointing shanks on to handles. There is a series of step-by-step guides on making a range of popular sticks using a variety of materials that will help beginners and experienced stickmakers who want to expand their stickmaking skills. The book is designed to assist people of all abilities to make a stick of their choice; it explains how to make a simple stick with a few basic tools, through to shaping buffalo horn, and bulking and dressing sheep horn to make a classic shepherd's crook, which is often regarded as the most difficult type of stick to make. The final chapter focuses on decorating handles using two completely different materials: timber and buffalo horn. The methods used can be applied to the other materials used in this book.

All the sticks featured in this guide have been made by the author using traditional materials. The techniques, jigs and tools used may differ from other stick dressers, but they are based on traditional methods. During my time making sticks I have received help and advice from many expert stick dressers, and I would like to thank all of them for willingly sharing their knowledge and experience with me. Without their help and encouragement I would not have gained the confidence required to write this book on such a fascinating and absorbing craft.

I hope you enjoy your stickmaking and find some of the information in this book helpful.

Charlie Walker

OPPOSITE: **A traditional market stick.**

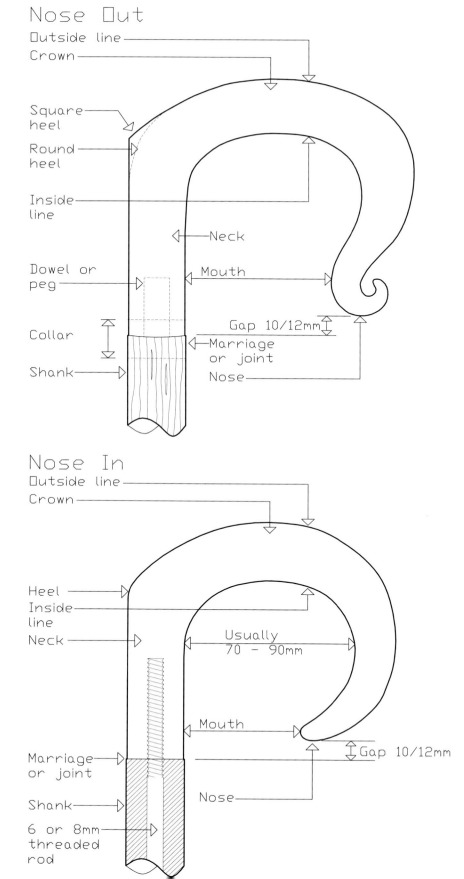

Nose Out

- Outside line
- Crown
- Square heel
- Round heel
- Inside line
- Neck
- Dowel or peg
- Mouth
- Collar
- Gap 10/12mm
- Marriage or joint
- Shank
- Nose

Nose In

- Outside line
- Crown
- Heel
- Inside line
- Neck
- Usually 70 – 90mm
- Mouth
- Gap 10/12mm
- Marriage or joint
- Nose
- Shank
- 6 or 8mm threaded rod

GETTING STARTED

When reading old stickmaking books and talking with stickmakers, especially the older generations, they often refer to the size of a stick in inches, even though we now live in the metric world. A conversion chart is useful, but to help a little, here are some measurements used in this book: please note they are rounded to the nearest number and are not mathematically exactly correct, but the tolerances quoted are acceptable.

¼in = 6mm; ⁵/₁₆in = 8mm; ³/₈in = 10mm; ½in = 12mm
1in = 25mm; 1¹/₈in = 30mm; 1¼in = 32mm
2in = 50mm; 6in = 150mm
36in = 915mm; 48in =1,220mm; 52in = 1,320mm

Basic Styles

Handles

The sketches show two common types of handle: the first is a traditional crook shape and is often referred to as a 'nose out' handle; the second shape is typically used for market and walking sticks, and is generally known as a 'nose in' handle. The parts identified in the sketches are used in the book to describe some of the steps used when making similar styles of handle. Different shapes and styles of handle are featured in the book, and the relevant parts are described.

Two of the most common methods of fixing stick handles to shanks are shown on the sketches, namely with a dowel joint and a stud joint using threaded rod, and both methods can be used on the sticks featured in this book; alternative methods of making joints are discussed in later chapters. The sketch also shows the ideal position of a collar when fitted to strengthen the joint between a handle and a shank.

In stickmaking there are no stringent measurements to adhere to: there are simply guidelines that give an idea of the size and shape of handles and the height of a stick. The reason that there are no set measurements is because people choose to use sticks of different weights, heights, styles and sizes; thus some people want a tall stick to use as a rifle rest, while others will opt for a shorter stick to provide support when resting during a long walk.

Variations in Style: Crooks

A good example of the variations in one style of stick is the crook; there are many shapes, such as a Brighton crook, a round heel crook,

OPPOSITE: **Stick shapes**

a Tam O'Shanter crook, a square heel crook, and a leg cleek, and some of these crooks will have a different type of nose, such as a half-curled nose, a curled nose, a looped nose and a decorated nose made on the crook. It would be impracticable to set measurements for the many variations of just one style of stick.

Crooks are made in different sizes because the individual maker's interpretation of a crook differs; also the end users will pick different sizes and shapes, as some shepherds prefer a short, light crook while others will choose a heavier and longer crook. Another factor to consider for a working crook is the breed and size of sheep it will have to handle, as sheep differ throughout the country, and shepherds will opt for a crook that is most suitable for use with their particular breed of sheep. Furthermore crooks are now used by some alpaca farmers, who use them to work with their animals.

A 'leg cleek' is a term used for a smaller crook, whose handle is shaped with a tighter gape than a full crook, and where the shank is often shorter than a standard crook; they are used to catch sheep and lambs by their legs when the shepherd wants to separate an individual sheep from the flock; some poultry farmers also use leg cleeks to catch geese and turkeys by their neck. Leg cleeks are the only sticks to have set measurements for the handle, and not all shepherds agree with these sizes; some believe the mouth is too small. The traditional measurement used for the mouth (gape) is an old halfpenny, and for the inside of the crown loop it is an old penny. These equate to 1in (25mm) for the mouth and 1¼in (30mm) for the inside of the loop; some judges continue to use these sizes when examining show sticks. Commercially made aluminium leg cleeks are often used as working sticks; the one featured has a mouth and loop of the same size, that is 1$\frac{1}{8}$in (27mm). Again this highlights how measurements can vary in the same type of stick.

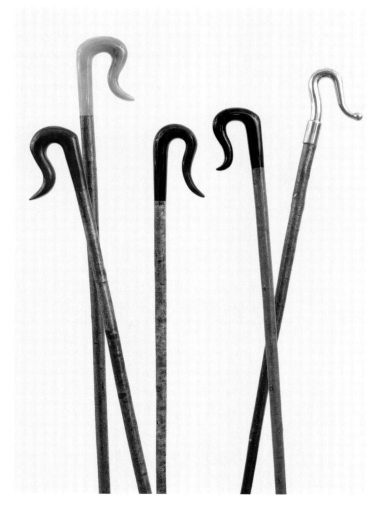

Leg cleeks.

Stick Height and Ferrules

Stick height differs according to individual preference, therefore stickmakers will often make a stick with a shank that is longer than normal, and will only shorten it and fit a ferrule when it is sold. The fitting of ferrules on exhibition sticks is a contentious issue: some judges regard a stick without a ferrule as being unfinished and will mark it down, while another judge understands why a ferrule is not fitted and will accept a stick without one. If a stick is exhibited with a ferrule, it should be well fitted on to the shank, as a badly fitted ferrule will downgrade the stick to the back of the stand – and it is surprising how often badly fitted ferrules are submitted in stick shows.

Some stickmakers make an adjustable stick to help people choose their preferred height before finally cutting a stick to length and fitting a ferrule; this is because once a stick is cut too short it cannot be successfully lengthened.

What Makes a Good Stick?

When making walking or working sticks the most important attributes to consider are these: it has to be functional and comfortable to use; it should feel balanced in the hand; and it must be well finished and have an excellent appearance. Everyone has a different interpretation of what makes a good stick, and even experienced show judges' opinions of sticks will differ – although they will all agree on certain standard requirements, such as:

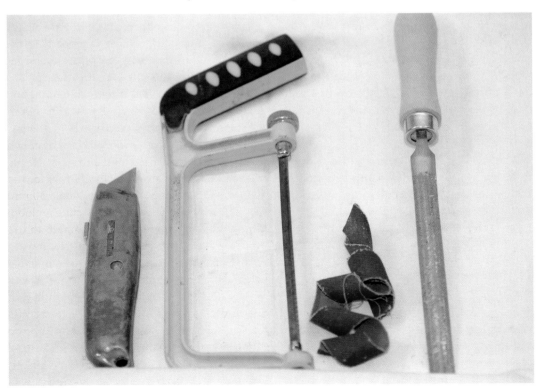

Basic tools.

- the stick must have a straight shank and a neat joint
- on most sticks the shank and handle should be aligned (there are some exceptions, such as curly and trout handles)
- the handle and shank should be balanced
- there must be no scratches, marks or defects on the handle or shank
- any decorations must be an accurate representation of the subject

These are standards that all stickmakers should strive to achieve, as they demonstrate that the maker is skilful, and makes good quality, reliable sticks.

Basic Tools

It is possible to make simple sticks with a few basic tools, the essentials being a sharp knife, a saw, a file and some abrasive cloth. A means of holding a stick while working on it is also helpful: a portable vice that clamps on to a table or a 'workmate' will get you started. A simple one-piece stick can be made with just these few basic tools.

When you start to make a wider range of sticks you will begin to build up a larger collection of tools and equipment; some of the most useful are described below.

Abrasives

Abrasives are used extensively in stickmaking to provide a smooth surface prior to applying a finish. There are several types and qualities of abrasive to choose from, and they are available in many forms, such as liquid, paste, paper, cloth, plastic, rolls, sheets, discs and wire wool. Abrasives are designed to be used by hand or

machine. Electrically or air-operated machines can be used to remove material quickly, and will save on time and effort, but they must be used with care as too much material can easily and quickly be removed by these machines.

Personal protective equipment (PPE) should always be worn when using any abrasive with powered machines to prevent grit and debris from causing harm or injury; it is essential to wear eye protection. Abrasives applied by hand require more effort and will be slower than using powered equipment, but the risk of mistakes will be significantly reduced, and your patience will be rewarded when using this method to produce a smooth, scratch-free surface.

Paper and Cloth Abrasives

Paper- and cloth-backed abrasives are number graded according to their 'grit', the lower numbers being the most aggressive grits and the higher numbers the least severe: for example 30 to 100 grit is coarse, 120 to 320 is medium, 400 to 800 is fine, and 1,000 and above is very fine.

Some abrasives are backed with Velcro, allowing them to be attached to a range of discs and pads so they can used by hand or machine. Flexible variations are useful for shaping curved and round surfaces, while rigid pads are good for smoothing flat surfaces and maintaining a sharp edge. Open-mesh abrasives that adhere to Velcro are popular because they do not choke up with dust as much as some paper and cloth abrasives; gently tapping the mesh on to a solid surface will remove most of the dust particles.

Velcro adhesive tape is readily available so anyone can make their own style and shape of sanding pads. Waterproof abrasive sheets, commonly known as 'wet' and 'dry', are used to provide a very smooth finish; the paper can be used dry, but is best used with a drop of water

MAKING A SIMPLE ONE-PIECE STICK

A simple staff or a thumb stick are good examples to begin with, as they will both make excellent, functional sticks that will last for years with a little care and attention.

Step 1: Cut a seasoned stick to length; if it is a forked thumb-stick, cut each finger to an identical length and smooth off the tips. They may be left flat or the edges can be slightly rounded if preferred. If it is a plain staff, smooth off the top, again slightly rounding the edges so it is comfortable to hold. Avoid using a bent shank. Seasoned shanks can be purchased from some of the suppliers listed if you do not have access to woodland or hedgerows where you can cut and collect your own shanks.

Step 2: Remove any offshoots and smooth them off with a file or abrasive paper. It is a personal choice whether they protrude a little, or are cut level to the shank.

Step 3: Fit a metal ferrule on the bottom tip; cut a short dowel on the bottom of the shank with the saw and knife, file the dowel so the ferrule fits snugly onto the shank and glue it in place to protect the end of the stick. A rubber ferrule can be used to slip over the shank if preferred; it should also be glued to hold it in position.

Step 4: Using abrasive paper, gently remove any loose bark and dirt, and finish the stick by applying oil suitable for outdoor use with a lint-free cloth. Allow the oil to dry, and apply further coats which will help to protect the stick and improve its appearance. Oil can be applied regularly to maintain a stick in good condition.

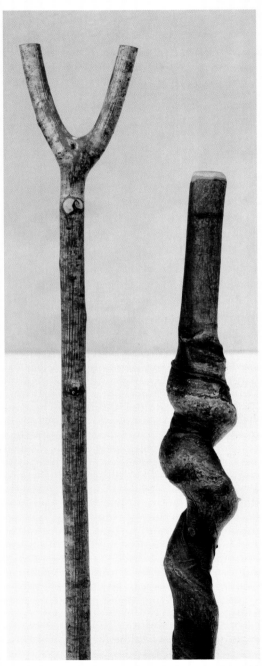

Thumb stick and staff.

which will make a fine abrasive paste when it is carefully rubbed on to a surface. The paper can be obtained in a range of grits up to 2,500 grit, which is extremely fine. Take care when using this type of abrasive on absorbent, pale-coloured surfaces as the dirt generated during the smoothing process may contaminate and discolour the material, especially pale-coloured wood.

Wire Wool

Wire wool is graded by a series of 0 (zeros): thus coarse wool is 0 rated, and 0000 is the finest. Wire wool works well when it is used with a liquid or paste abrasive, and will provide an excellent surface prior to applying a finish. Wire wool can also be used to apply oils, giving a lovely sheen to the surface of timbers and horn. It is also used to de-nib (remove the gloss from) a finish from a varnish or lacquer so that additional coats can be applied if required. It is often used to make a smooth matt finish, which some people prefer. A word of caution: wire wool will rust if exposed to wet conditions, so it is important to ensure that all wire particles are removed from the surface of your stick before applying a final finish.

Liquid Abrasives

Liquid abrasives are used to remove very fine scratches and marks; some are designed for use on vehicles and metals, however they can be used on a range of stickmaking materials such as horn, metal collars and ferrules. A popular black abrasive used for vehicles and known as T Cut is useful for smoothing buffalo horn, as the black dye is absorbed into the material, which helps to darken some of the natural markings that occur in buffalo horns. Liquid abrasives do not work so well on timber as the dirt gener-

ated can be absorbed in the grain of the timber, so always test these on a similar piece of material before using on your chosen project.

Files, Rasps and Rifflers

Files, rasps and rifflers are useful for shaping most of the materials used in stickmaking.

Files

Files are generally used for engineering work on metals; however, they will cut most materials and are useful for working horn and antler, though the teeth may become clogged when used on some soft materials such as timber. A wire brush will remove most of the debris from a file.

Files are graded according to their coarseness: thus bastard cut files are the most severe, progressing to 2nd cut and down to smooth. They are available in a many shapes and sizes – flat, half round, round, square and three-cornered – and in a variety of lengths, from 12in (30cm) down to 4in (10cm) in the standard ranges, and they are sold individually or in sets. Sets of miniature, midget and needle files are also available for very fine work.

Rasps

Rasps are similar to files, but the teeth are designed to work best on softer materials such as timber, leather, horn and animal hoofs, as they are less likely to choke during use. Farriers use a large, double-sided rasp to file back a horse's hoof during the trimming or reshoeing process, and similarly rasps are excellent for removing waste material from cow and sheep horn. It is well worth buying good quality files and rasps as they will retain their sharpness longer than inferior quality ones, which soon lose their edge.

Woodworking rasps are made especially for removing waste from timbers, and using them on metal must be avoided. Traditional surform and modern stainless-steel rasps are used because they are very sharp and leave a reasonably smooth surface on the timber. These rasps are available in a variety of shapes and sizes, and some models allow blades to be interchanged with a single handle.

Japanese double-sided rasps are popular as they will cut most stickmaking materials such as horn, plastics and timber, and the blade is so designed that it does not clog up during use.

Rifflers

A riffler is a type of rasp used to shape materials in difficult places on a carving. Most rifflers are double-ended, and the end sections are made in various shapes and profiles so the riffler can reach into the most awkward situations, enabling detailed shapes to be made in tricky positions. They are very useful for stickmakers who decorate handles as they will cut horn and timber, and will survive for a time if used on antler. Rifflers are normally sold in sets, and the cost varies depending on the size and quality of the tool.

Adhesives

There are numerous types of adhesive available for general and specialist applications: some are waterproof, some stick on impact, while others set slowly. A few adhesives are made for specific applications and materials, and will not adhere to any other surfaces or materials,

so always read the manufacturer's instructions before using a product to ensure it is suitable for a particular application.

Popular epoxy resins require mixing: they usually come in two equal parts, and are popular with stickmakers as they provide a strong bond and can be used on most of the materials used in stickmaking. Thus they will successfully glue together timber, antler and horn, and many other materials. They are available in small or large quantities, with setting times that vary from five minutes to several hours, making them very versatile for stickmaking.

Polyvinyl acetate (PVA) is an adhesive formulated principally for use with timber: it is strong and waterproof, and is ideal for use with wooden sticks. Some timbers require specific adhesives because of their oil and chemical content, so when using exotic woods or some hardwoods check the suitability of the product before use.

Cyanoacrylates, commonly known as 'superglues', are available in a range of thicknesses and setting times from instant to several minutes. Thin superglues can be used for strengthening timber and horns as they penetrate deep into the fibre of the material, while the thicker types can be used to fill small gaps. Superglues must be used with care as some types will instantly bond skin together, so precautions must be in place to ensure they do not come into contact with eyes and fingers. It is advisable to have a de-bonding solution at hand when using cyanoacrylates, which can be applied in the event of an incident occurring.

Fillers

Two-part fillers can be obtained in various colours, and may be used for example to set eyes into carved bird and animal heads, as the coloured background is effective when used with some species. Filler is also sometimes used to fill voids and gaps when they appear, as it

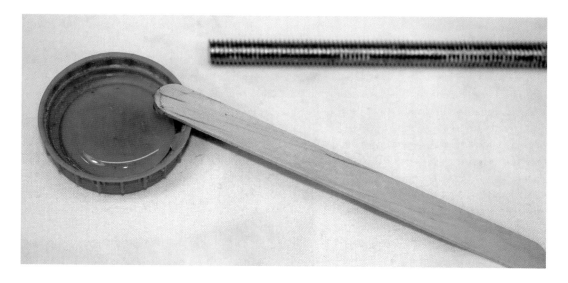

A lid and lollipop stick.

can be smoothed with files and abrasives and then covered with paint, as, for example, on a decorated handle.

Always check the manufacturer's instructions because most fillers and adhesives have to be used within a particular temperature range, and some set very slowly or may not set at all if the temperature is too low.

Lids from empty jars and milk containers are ideal for mixing small quantities of two-part adhesives, fillers and paints, as they save making a mess on your work table or bench and can be thrown away after use. Packs of lollipop sticks can be purchased from craft shops and are ideal for mixing epoxy glues; their straight edges are also perfect for aligning handles and shanks.

Types of Finish

Before applying a finish it is advisable to seal shanks and wooden handles; several types of sealer are available, and they are often referred to as sanding sealers. Cellulose and acrylic sealers are popular, and can be applied by brush,

with a cloth, or by aerosol spray. The sealer is applied, and when it has dried it can be rubbed down with a fine abrasive, making a perfect surface for a finishing product. Several coats can be used if necessary.

It is good practice to apply a finish to a stick, as it will help to protect and preserve it for many years. There is a huge range of finishes to choose from, though be aware that some are designed for interior use only and are not suitable for outdoor applications. Suitable finishes are acrylic-, cellulose-, spirit- and water-based lacquers and varnishes, and these are available in a gloss, satin or matt finish, depending on individual choice. There are stains, paints, varnishes, oils and waxes on the open market that are suitable, and all stickmakers have their preferred brands and types.

It is very important when applying a finish to ensure that it is compatible with the sealer or base coat, as spirit- or cellulose-based lacquers and varnishes may cause a reaction if applied over acrylic- or water-based products. Always check the manufacturer's instructions before use, and if there is any doubt try the products on a small test area first.

Lacquer

Lacquers are generally fast setting and can be applied by brush, with a cloth, or from a spray can. They are available in gloss, satin and matt finishes. Because they are fast setting, additional coats can be applied to the surface in a short period if required. Some lacquers can be applied over paints and stains to provide protection, but always ensure that the lacquer is compatible with the colouring material before applying, and also that it is suitable for outdoor use.

Varnish

Varnishes generally take longer to dry than lacquers, and should be applied in a warm, dry and clean environment. Some experienced stickmakers thin the varnish as they prefer to use several thin coats rather than a single thick coat. When completely dry, each coat can be very lightly de-nibbed with very fine wire wool or wet and dry abrasives to give a key for the next coat. Several coats may be required to achieve a satisfactory finish, but take care when applying each one as the varnish may run if applied too thickly; furthermore, thickly applied varnish may also chip off in later use. Water- and spirit-based varnishes are available, and some are suitable for outdoor use.

Oil

Oils are a traditional and proven method of finishing sticks. There are several types of oil available for outdoor use, and those most commonly used by stickmakers are linseed, Danish, teak, tung and outdoor furniture oil. Be careful when selecting oil as some brands are only suitable for indoor applications.

Oils are popular because they soak into the timber, which helps to protect and waterproof the wood. However, be aware that oil takes longer to soak into timber and dry than lacquers and varnishes, so it may take a while to apply several coats. When oil is completely dry it can be burnished, and a pleasant sheen finish achieved. Oils can be over-coated regularly to maintain a protective finish.

Oil is an excellent choice for a walking or working stick that is used frequently in all weathers.

Paint

Paints are used to provide a coloured decoration on a handle, or to infill pyrography work or carvings; it is rarely used as the prime method of protecting the wood in stickmaking. There are several types of paint available that are suitable for decorating sticks; model and acrylic paints are among the most popular. Always use compatible finishes to protect painted surfaces, as some finishes may react adversely when used on top of paint.

Stain

Stains can improve the appearance of a shank with or without bark, and will often enhance knots, grains or blemishes that occur naturally in the wood. But a word of warning: stains will also highlight any defects in the wood, such as scratches or file marks, so ensure the surface is sound before applying them. Stains are best used on untreated timber as they soak deep into the grain, giving a long-lasting colour.

Most stains are spirit- or water-based, and it is important to remember which type you have used so you can select a compatible protective finish that will not react with the stain. Note that if stain is applied to dry timber it is likely to run along the grain of the wood, making it difficult to control if a fine edge is required. Also if it is intended to use a range of stains to colour a piece of timber such as a bird's head, use the lightest colours before applying the dark colours, as a pale-coloured stain will seldom cover a dark colour even if several coats are used.

It is advisable to test stains on a similar type of timber first to ensure the result meets your requirements, as it can be difficult to obtain the correct colour and shade. Compatible stains can be mixed to provide a wide range of colours, and it is advisable to keep a record of the mixing ratio used if you want to copy the colour at a later time.

Stains are best used for general colouring as they are difficult to control on intricate work or carvings.

Polish

Wax polish can be used as a final finish: it will give a lovely sheen and feel to a handle or shank, and will provide limited protection to your stick; however, it will wear off if a stick is used regularly in outdoor conditions. But as with oils, it is easily over-coated, and if applied regularly a beautiful finish can be maintained. Beeswax and microcrystalline polish work well when applied on to a finished surface, as do some liquid polishes used principally for vehicles and metals. Burnishing creams can be used to revive an old polish.

Top Tools

When setting up a workshop there are a few important tools that should be considered, some of which are listed below.

Vices

A strong, fixed vice should be among your top items if you are setting up a workshop. Vices that can be used for making sticks are available in many types and sizes. For example, mechanics' vices are strong and sturdy, and are normally bolted on top of a workbench, whereas woodworking vices are usually bolted on to the side of a workbench, leaving a flat worktop; these are available in different sizes. Swivel-headed vices are useful, especially for carving and shaping handles; some have shaped jaws that are ideal for holding shanks. Portable vices can be clamped on to a flat surface such as a table or workmate, and are useful when working away from home.

Select a good quality vice that can also be used for other jobs; for example, mechanics' vices make useful general purpose tools, and while the larger ones are heavy and expensive, they are ideal for making horn handles.

Hammers and Mallets

A selection of hammers is an essential part of any toolkit. The three most common types are claw hammers, which can also be used to pull out nails; ball-pein hammers are used mainly in engineering work and are useful for most jobs; while cross-pein hammers are ideal for driving in smaller nails and pins. Most hammers are described and sold by their weight; for example, a 4oz cross-pein hammer is used for delicate work, while a 1½lb claw hammer is used for general joinery work, and a 2lb ball-pein hammer is generally used for heavy engineering work. A 1½lb claw or ball-pein hammer will be a good choice for stickmaking.

Wooden mallets and soft-faced hammers are designed to reduce the risk of damage to all types of surface; they are often used in conjunction with wood-working and carving chisels to prevent the chisel handles from being damaged.

Drilling Machines, Twist Drills and Bits

Hand drills are not as popular as they used to be a few years ago; battery and mains electrically powered drills have taken over, and many now incorporate screwdrivers and hammers, making them extremely versatile. However, there are times when a hand drill or a brace and bit is useful when making a stick.

Battery drills are useful tools as they can be used in remote locations, and their low voltage makes them safe to use outdoors in wet conditions. Manufacturers now supply up to three spare batteries which can be recharged within an hour, giving virtually constant use if required. More and more professional builders and tradespeople are using heavy duty battery-operated drills because they are so flexible and operate without the need for a fixed power supply.

Bench and floor-standing pedestal drills are a good option in a workshop if you have the space, as they can be set up to drill very accurately, which is important when drilling out a stick handle.

Twist Drills and Bits
Twist drills, bits and augers are used for drilling and boring holes of different sizes in a wide variety of materials. Like most other tools, some are designed for a specific task while others can be used for general purpose work. A set of good quality, general purpose twist drills ranging from 1mm to 13mm will cover most stickmaking requirements as they will drill timber, horn, antler and steel.

Flat spade bits are intended for cutting holes in timber and are available in a range of sizes; they are ideal for cutting the 'pith' out of

antlers ready for jointing. A blunt spade bit will tear timber, therefore always keep them sharp. They can be purchased individually if you don't require a full set.

Forstner bits are designed to cut clean, accurate holes, making them a perfect choice for drilling holes into wooden handles ready for jointing. They can be obtained in sets or individually.

Auger bits are designed for cutting deep, accurate holes in timber, and can be used to drill the holes in shanks and handles.

Saws

Hacksaw frames will accept a range of blades that will cut most materials, especially metals and plastics. A junior hacksaw is most useful for smaller applications and will cut steel, plastics and timber; it is very useful when fitting ferrules and cutting dowel joints.

Coping saws are designed for cutting shapes. They will cut a tight bend in most materials with the correct blade inserted into the frame, and are particularly useful for cutting wood and horn handles. The thin blade performs best when used on the pull stroke, rather than pushing the blade into the material.

Tenon and dovetail saws are used for accurate cutting, and will make a neat cut when joining handles and shanks together.

Japanese saws are becoming popular as they are good quality and are very sharp, giving clean cuts; this makes them the ideal tool for accurate joints. Some of these saws have interchangeable blades for different materials and cuts.

A **mitre saw** is designed to cut accurate angles, and is useful for cutting a sloping joint or straight joint between a handle and shank. They are also used extensively for picture framing.

A **universal handsaw** will cut sheets and planks of timber, and a range of soft materials such as plastics and man-made boards; it is an excellent tool for general use.

A folding **pruning saw** is ideal for cutting green shanks and branches if you intend to cut and collect your own shanks, while a large, sharp pruning saw will cut through a thick branch if you want to cut your own block sticks.

Electric jigsaws will cut shapes up to 2in (50mm) deep in a range of materials with the appropriate blade, and are capable of cutting wooden blanks for stick handles from planked timber.

If space is available, a **bandsaw** is ideal for stickmaking; it will cut tight curves in 6in (150mm) blocks of timber at various angles, and with an appropriate blade fitted it will cut most stickmaking materials. They are expensive, but are a most useful tool, especially if other DIY work is undertaken in the workshop.

Obtaining Tools

As with most hobbies, the number of tools you obtain will increase as you become more involved, and stickmaking is no exception. Tools can be purchased from a huge range of suppliers and manufacturers: the choice is massive, so choose carefully and buy the best quality you can afford, as they will last longer than inferior versions.

If cost is an issue, good quality second-hand tools can be found at car boot sales and second-hand shops at a fraction of the new price. They are frequently advertised in local newspapers and magazines.

Ideas and Inspiration

Having obtained sufficient tools to get started, it is time for ideas and inspiration as to the type and style of sticks to make. It is to be hoped that this book will give anyone new to stickmaking some ideas and options. If readers want to be more adventurous and carve animals, birds or fish, there are various ways of obtaining pictures and photos. Specialist books on carving animals and birds are available, with detailed drawings and sketches, which can be used to make a range of handles. Magazines, newspapers and other media often have pictures of animals and birds that can be used, and hundreds of excellent photos can be found on internet sites and downloaded for personal use.

One of the best ways to obtain your own pictures is to visit game fairs, country and agricultural shows, zoos and farms, where you can take several photos of a subject from different angles so that the position of eyes, ears, mouth and nose, and the colouring, can be accurately reproduced on your stick handle. Modern digital cameras and telephones are ideal for taking photos, as the images can be easily and cheaply downloaded and printed at home.

Modern photocopiers are capable of increasing or reducing the size of pictures to scale, allowing a stickmaker to make an appropriately sized picture: this can be transferred on to a blank by tracing the outline using carbon paper, or by cutting sections of the picture that can be glued on to a blank, making it easy to mark out all the main features of the object so an accurate replica can be made.

Joining a local or national stickmaking organization with like-minded members is a good way of obtaining ideas, inspiration and help. There are some incredibly clever and talented people making sticks, and probably there will be a club quite close to you with several members who make fantastic sticks, and who will be more than willing to help and give advice to any new member. Most clubs place information on the internet about themselves, with contact details for anyone wishing to inquire about membership.

**Examples of
suitable timbers
for stickmaking.**

SELECTING, STORING, STRAIGHTENING AND JOINTING TIMBER

There is a huge variety of timber available for stickmaking. Some timbers are suitable for making shanks, while others are best for fashioning handles, and all experienced stickmakers have their preferred types and species. An ideal shank needs to be light, strong, straight, durable and attractive; timber for handles has to be strong, durable and attractive. Close-grained timbers are best for handles, as they will withstand the wear and tear of a working stick better than open-grained timbers, which may break or crack when subjected to the arduous duties expected from a stick. Some popular timbers are listed below, but there are many other native and exotic timbers that can be used, and it is well worth experimenting, especially when making handles.

If you intend to cut timber from woodland or hedgerows, remember to obtain permission from the landowner first.

Popular Timbers

Ash

Ash makes sturdy shanks, but the bark is uninteresting, so stickmakers often remove the

OPPOSITE: **Some potential shanks.**

outer bark with a scraper or wire wool, revealing the more colourful inner bark: this can be enhanced by coating it with stain.

Planked ash will make good, serviceable stick handles, but ensure the grain is running in the correct direction, otherwise the wood may crack if dropped on to a hard floor.

Birch

Young silver birch branches are coloured brown, which turn paler when the tree matures. The bark eventually turns a silver colour and can be easily pealed from the tree. Young birch shoots make attractive shanks that are both light and strong. Mature birch makes good handles.

Blackthorn

Blackthorn is regarded by many stickmakers as one of the best woods to use for shanks because of its strength, colour and knotted appearance. It is difficult and quite dangerous to cut as it is covered with sharp thorns that are poisonous, so ensure you wear appropriate protection; if your skin is punctured it is advisable to seek medical attention.

Blackthorn is used to make knob sticks and cudgels; in Ireland these are known as 'shillelaghs' and were originally used as throwing sticks to down small game.

Shanks with regularly spaced knots are the

most sought after, and excellent one-piece cross-handled sticks can be made by digging up a root with the shank still intact.

Blackthorn needs to be seasoned slowly in a dry, cool environment to minimize the risk of shakes (small cracks) appearing in the surface.

Chestnut (Sweet)

Thousands of sticks are made annually for the NHS using sweet chestnut. When steamed it can be bent easily and is often used to make one-piece crooks, as well as the short walking sticks issued by the NHS for the infirm. It is a strong and versatile wood that makes good shanks.

Fruitwoods

Fruitwoods such as cherry, crab apple, apple, pear and wild plum make attractive shanks, although thinner shanks may be too weak to provide adequate support for the user. Some shanks are heavily knotted and have a rich colouring, giving them a lot of character, which makes them a popular choice. Excellent handles can be made from larger sections of fruitwood.

Hawthorn

Hawthorn makes strong, heavy shanks but the bark is quite plain in colour, and stickmakers often strip the bark from the shank and colour the wood with stain or by fuming. Like blackthorn, it is covered with thorns making it difficult to cut, but it is not as poisonous, although the thorns can penetrate quite deeply causing severe pain – so again use appropriate protection.

Hazel

Hazel is the most popular wood used by stickmakers as it is light, strong, colourful and plentiful; also the shoots grow fairly straight, making excellent shanks. The bark varies considerably from plain silver and brown to heavily mottled in colour, and unlike in some woods, the bark is seldom removed because it is so attractive. Large hazel branches with a suitable offshoot are frequently used to make one-piece sticks.

Holly

Holly is a dense timber that makes heavy sticks; the bark has a tendency to wrinkle during the seasoning period, so most stickmakers will strip it off once the shank is fully seasoned. It is recommended that the bark is left in place until then, otherwise the shank may split. When the bark is removed the shank is a pale colour, which can be given a beautiful finish, especially when the knots are left to protrude slightly. The stripped wood can be stained if a coloured finish is preferred. Holly should be given more time to season than most woods, in a cool dry place. Thick branches can be reduced in diameter, often revealing attractive patterns in the heartwood.

Timber for Handles

Handles are best made from close-grained timbers because they are stronger than when made from soft, open-grained timbers, as these can break if dropped on to a hard surface or put under too much strain during use. Several British and imported timbers can be used to make beautiful handles, and are available in suitably sized planks from timber suppliers. Exotic timbers can be purchased from specialist timber merchants if a really unique handle is required.

Interesting handles can be obtained by cutting unusually shaped branches and roots from a variety of woods such as blackthorn, box, broom, ivy, rhododendron and privet; it is well worth experimenting with a range of timbers.

Equipment for cutting shanks.

Cutting Shanks

Many stickmakers prefer to cut their own shanks from hedgerows, coppices and woods during the winter months when the sap is at its lowest, especially in deciduous trees, although most stickmakers will cut a stick when they find it; if it is left it can be difficult to find again – or even worse, someone else may find it and take it home!

Shanks from evergreen trees are usually cut after they have fruited, again when the sap is reputed to be at its lowest. However, shanks can be cut at any time of the year providing they are given sufficient time to dry out and season. Always cut your shanks longer and slightly thicker than required for your finished stick, as the diameter of the wood will shrink as it dries, and shakes (small cracks) may appear in the ends if it is dried too quickly. Do not cut offshoots or thorns too close to the unseasoned shank as shakes may appear as the stick dries.

The tools required to cut shanks are a folding pruning saw to cut branches, a pair of secateurs to cut offshoots, a pair of gloves to protect your hands, and a ball of string or a couple of leather straps (dog collars are good) to tie your sticks in a bundle.

When a stick has been fully seasoned it can be prepared to make a shank: the length can be reduced and the knots cut closer. Shanks of 1in (25mm) or less in diameter will season in about twelve months, but it is recommended to let

them thoroughly dry out for two or more years before use.

Storing Shanks

Shanks should be stored in a cool, dry environment with sufficient space to allow a free flow of air around them. It is recommended that they are treated regularly against woodworm by dipping both ends in a bucket of solution, and spraying or wiping the shank with a proven product. For best results it is recommended that shanks are treated twice a year, but ensure they are treated at least annually to prevent infestation.

The life cycle of these pests is three to four years: the fly lays her eggs in tiny cracks and crevices in springtime, and when they hatch, the minute grubs eat their way into the timber; they may stay inside it for several years before emerging, leaving a tell-tale hole – and there is no way of telling if a tiny grub has entered the wood until it emerges. During this time it will have eaten its way along a substantial section of the timber, rendering it useless. After the grub has emerged it hatches out into a fly, and the whole process begins again.

Thus a grub may be in the wood before it is used, which is why woodworm holes some-

Shank store.

times appear after a stick has been finished and varnished, especially if it has not been treated with a woodworm killer during storage. If several eggs were laid it is probable that numerous grubs will be active in the timber, rendering it useless, as they will tunnel along the complete length of the shank.

Store shanks in the order of the year they are cut, and use the oldest first. Store them in bundles or racks making sure there is sufficient space to allow fresh air to circulate around them to aid the drying process.

Straightening Shanks

Only shanks that are fully seasoned should be straightened. It is a waste of time trying to straighten a green, unseasoned shank as it will always try to revert back to its original shape.

To straighten a shank, each bent section has to be heated, and there are two types of heat that may be used: dry or wet. Heat is applied to the shank until it becomes pliable, and at this point the bent part of the shank can be gently forced in the opposite direction of the bend in a jig or over your knee until it is straight; the section of shank is then allowed to cool

for a few minutes. If there are more bends to straighten along the shank these are heated and straightened in the same manner. It may take more than one session to get a perfectly straight shank. The same technique and jigs are used for both wet and dry heat.

Straightening board and jig.

Dry Heat

Dry heat is usually achieved by using an electric hot-air gun as used by decorators for removing paints and varnishes. Gas torches or blowlamps can be used, but there is greater risk of scorching or burning the timber with a naked flame unless the bark is protected with aluminium foil. Hot-air guns with variable temperature controls are best; they are usually rated between 1 and 2kw.

When using a hot-air gun, keep it moving across the wood to allow the heat to penetrate into the fibres, and also to prevent it from scorching the wood, which should be hot to the touch. Hot-air guns can be purchased from most hardware and DIY shops. The main advantage of using a hot-air gun is that the heat can be directed on to a specific part of the shank;

Steam pipe.

they are used by stickmakers who want a perfectly straight shank.

Placing a shank directly on top of a hot domestic heating radiator can provide sufficient heat to soften some type of shank if there is no other option. However, it is not the best method, and is not recommended.

Wet Heat

There are three ways of treating a shank with wet heat: the first is to immerse it in boiling water; the second is to use steam to heat it; and the third is to submerge it in a bed of hot wet sand. Few stickmakers have a container large enough to immerse a complete shank in boiling water, and only commercial stickmakers use beds of hot wet sand, therefore amateur stickmakers generally use one of the steam methods, as described below.

A section of a shank can be heated if it is held directly over the spout of a boiling kettle or an open pan or urn. Some stickmakers wrap the stick with cloth so the steam heats the cloth, which in turn transfers the heat into the shank; it is then straightened as described above.

If several shanks are to be straightened in a session, a container can be made to hold a number of sticks, and a supply of steam fed in from a wallpaper stripping machine. A lidded timber box or a piece of heavy duty plastic pipe can be used to hold several sticks.

The simple container shown in the illustration is made from a piece of 4in- (10cm-) diameter plastic pipe with a thick wall. The pipe is attached to a baseboard with two shelving brackets, and a hole is cut into the bottom so the hose of a wallpaper stripping machine can be inserted. **Note that if the steam is sealed in the container it will explode, so always allow the steam to vent freely into the atmosphere.** The container in the illustration will hold about eight shanks at a time, which is an advantage if you want to straighten several shanks in a session.

Steam the shanks for about ten minutes, and then begin the straightening process using a straightening jig or block; the remaining shanks can be safely left in the container, and when you remove a shank it can be replaced with another. A long shank may have to turned and heated at the other end if the pipe is too short to heat the whole length.

After the steaming process it is likely that to make a perfectly straight shank some 'fine tuning' will be required using a hot-air gun, as its heat can be directed on to a specific section of the shank. Applying heat, especially by steaming the whole shank, will also kill any bugs and woodworm that may have burrowed into the timber.

Prepared Shanks

If you do not have the equipment or facilities to cut, store and straighten your own shanks, prepared and fully seasoned shanks that have been straightened can be obtained from commercial suppliers (*see* Further Information).

Jointing Shanks

Joints have to be made on each end of a shank, at the top to fasten a handle, and at the bottom to fix a ferrule to protect the working end of a shank. Joints are very important in stickmaking as they must be strong enough to hold the handle in position, and be capable of coping with the stress of a person or animal leaning, pulling and twisting against it with considerable force. The joint that fastens the ferrule must also be strong and well fitted so it will survive all types of weather and ground conditions that it is subjected to during its lifetime. A badly fitted joint will not only spoil the appearance of a stick, but may affect its functionality, which on a working stick is important as it must be a dependable and trustworthy tool for its user.

The appearance of a joint is important as it demonstrates the level of care and attention the maker takes when making a stick: thus a badly fitting joint immediately reveals to a potential buyer that the maker is careless and their workmanship is shoddy, whereas a well-fitted joint shows that the maker is careful and attentive to detail, so their stick will probably be well made and reliable.

Types of Joint

There are four methods that are commonly used to joint handles on to shanks; they are as follows:

Method One: A dowel is made on a shank and a suitably sized hole is drilled into a handle;

the dowel is then glued into the handle. Some stickmakers drill a 3mm hole into the dowel and then glue a 3 × 75mm long galvanized masonry nail into the dowel to increase the strength of the joint. The joint is permanent.

A dowel is cut on a shank.

Method Two: Some stickmakers prefer to use a turned hardwood dowel that is inserted and glued into suitably sized holes that have been drilled in both the shank and handle. A masonry nail can be used (as described above) if required. This method is often used to joint an antler head on to a shank. The joint is permanent.

A separate hardwood dowel.

Method Three: A length of rod is used, and inserted and glued into suitably sized holes drilled into the shank and the handle: 6mm or 8mm threaded steel rod is mostly used for these joints. Some stickmakers use carbon fibre or aluminium rods to reduce the weight of the joint, especially on lightweight exhibition sticks. The joint is permanent.

Studding glued into a handle.

Method Four: Threaded inserts can be fitted into the handle or shank: they come in two sizes, 6mm and 8mm, and they require a larger hole to be drilled into the handle or shank – for example, a 6mm insert will require an 8mm hole to be drilled. The insert is glued and then screwed into the hole using an Allen key. There are also two types of insert: one is flanged, while the other is not, thus allowing it to be sunk deeper into the hole. A length of threaded rod to match the thread of the insert is fitted and glued into the handle or shank, leaving a short length protruding to screw into the insert.

It is important that both the insert and threaded rod are positioned so the handle and shank are perfectly aligned, and the joint is a tight fit with no gaps evident before gluing. When the glue has set in the handle and shank they can be screwed tightly together.

The advantage of this method is that the handle can be removed; it also allows handles and shanks to be interchanged if required. In the illustration the insert is fitted on to a shank.

A threaded insert.

Fitting a Ferrule

To fit a ferrule, a dowel is made on the end of the shank to match the size and shape of the ferrule; there must be a smooth transition between the ferrule and shank. A tight-fitting joint is best between the ferrule and shank to prevent water ingress: the ferrule is glued on the shank, and it is recommended that the end of the shank is smeared with adhesive to reduce the risk of water entering into the shank. Some stickmakers prefer to pin the ferrule, while others use a centre punch to put three equally spaced indents around the ferrule to help it grip on to the shank.

A correctly fitted ferrule is important because it is the working end of the stick and is subjected to all the rigours of different weather and ground conditions.

A fitted ferrule.

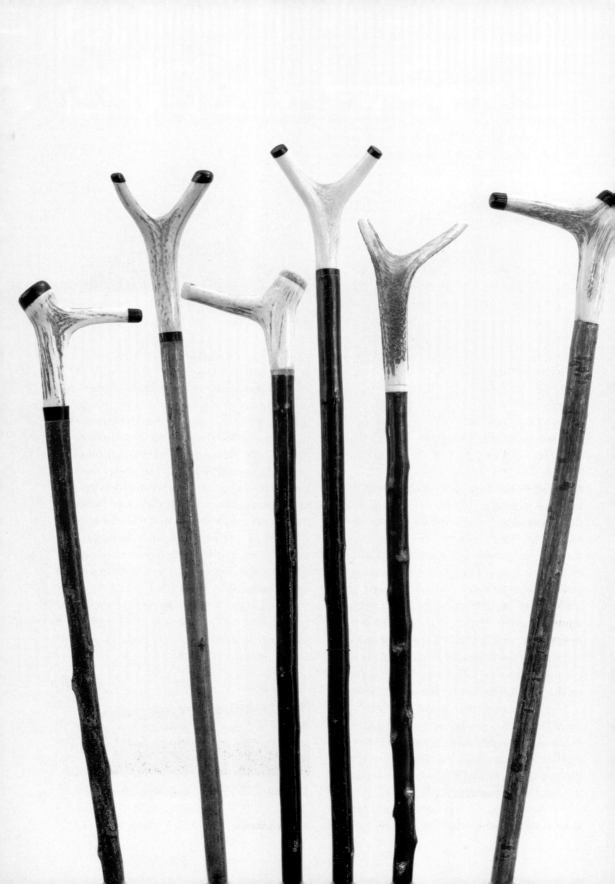

ANTLER HANDLES

Antler makes excellent handles, and it is relatively easy to make a strong, hard-wearing and attractive stick with a few good quality tools. Antler is a popular choice, and many people are eager to own a stick made from this natural material.

Deer cast their antlers once a year, generally in spring except for roe deer, which cast theirs in autumn. Cast-off antlers are difficult to find in the open countryside, although experienced rangers know the best places to find them. However, wild deer are increasing in parts of the country, and the herds are causing so much damage to woodland and crops that they are being culled in order to contain their numbers to a manageable level. Deer stalking remains popular throughout the UK, but particularly in the large estates of the Scottish Highlands and Islands, where the sport is a major contributor to the local economies. Gamekeepers and rangers who manage the herds of deer select old, injured or those in poor condition to be shot during the authorized shooting seasons, and these antlers are a major source of material for stickmakers.

Also, the popularity of venison meat is increasing, so deer farming has expanded, increasing the number of animals in the country, which in turn makes more antlers available for stickmakers. However, antler is used in many other industries and hobbies, and more recently it is sought by dog owners, who buy it for 'dog chews': this sudden demand has considerably increased its cost, making antler-handled sticks more expensive.

The size and thickness of antlers both vary according to the age of the animal; its location and feeding habits also contribute to the growth rate of its antlers. There is evidence to suggest that where grazing is sparse, the antlers grow more slowly and thicker than in animals reared on lush grazing, where the antler grows faster, resulting in thinner walls. The smaller, thicker-walled antlers are best for stickmaking, and are generally found in wild deer that roam over the remote countryside, rather than farmed deer contained in parkland. Large trophy antlers can often be seen prominently displayed in grand houses and hotels, and can be found at auction and in salerooms – but a word of caution before you are tempted to buy, as these are often too big for stickmaking: so don't be too envious when you look at these impressive specimens.

The surface and colour of antlers both vary considerably: some are very rough to the touch, while others are quite smooth, and the colours range from very dark to pale, depending on where the animals graze. Dirty antlers can be cleaned with soap and water using a stiff brush, which can significantly change their appearance, and an antler soaked for a few days in thin bleach will turn out to be almost white.

Many people prefer rough, dark-coloured antlers because they are more 'rustic' than

OPPOSITE: **Antler handles.**

some of the smoother, paler ones; however, they can be uncomfortable to hold, especially for long periods of time. The roughness can be smoothed a little with files or abrasives without affecting the character too much, making the handle more comfortable in use, which is important in a working stick.

Deer Species

There are four main species of wild deer roaming around the United Kingdom, namely fallow, red, roe and sika, and they all grow antlers that can be used by stickmakers with varying degrees of success.

Fallow Deer

Fallow deer are widespread in England and Wales, and can often be seen grazing leisurely in large parks. They are the only breed to have palmate antlers, and while the palmate section is of little use to stickmakers, the antler can produce a coronet and tine that will make a suitable handle, and occasionally a decent thumb stick can be obtained from these antlers. The palmate section can be used to make spacers or to mount candle holders, or for clocks and barometers, so do not discard them.

Red Deer

Red deer are common in Scotland, the Lake District, East Anglia, the New Forest and the South West of England, and they are steadily spreading into other regions. Their antlers make excellent handles and are used regularly by stickmakers. They are readily available, although the price is steadily increasing due to demand from dog owners who are buying them for their pets to chew.

Antlers from different breeds.

Roe Deer

Roe deer are widespread and roe deer antlers are plentiful, but they are small. The surface of the antler is very rough and sharp, making them uncomfortable to hold. Small thumb sticks can be made from them, but it is difficult to make a neat joint between the antler and shank.

Sika Deer

Sika deer are widespread in Scotland but their distribution is patchy in England, although their numbers are increasing in some counties. The size of sika deer is in between the red and roe species, and their antlers are smaller and have eight points. The antlers are more difficult to obtain than those of red deer, but they make decent handles so if the opportunity arises, try to obtain some. The illustration shows antlers from different breeds of deer.

Other Species

Reindeer and a few other species can be found in private herds, parks and zoos, but obtaining their antlers is difficult. Antler imported from the Indian Samba deer is regarded by many as the best because it has little or no pith, but it is difficult to obtain suitable pieces for stickmaking due to import restrictions.

Selecting Antler

When choosing an antler, select one with a thick wall so there is sufficient material to shape it on to the shank, making a smooth joint. The shape and size of the antler you choose must match the shank so the result is a nicely balanced stick; avoid fitting a heavy antler on to a light shank, or vice versa. The ideal thumb-stick handle is one that can be used in either hand and in both forward and reverse directions, but because of the way that antlers grow on the stag's head, this desirable shape can be difficult to find. Perfectly acceptable thumb-stick handles can be made from antlers that do not meet these criteria.

Antler Whistles

Do not throw away discarded antler tips as they make excellent whistles. The solid end prevents any air passing right through the tip when it

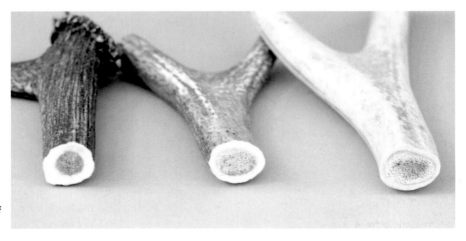

Various thicknesses of antler.

SAFETY WITH ANTLERS

Antler points can be very sharp and should be removed from any handle as they may cause a serious injury if the user trips and falls on to the point. Gamekeepers and rangers responsible for safety during planned shoots now ban antler handles with sharp points because of the risk of injury.

is blown, so it is all diverted past the reed and through the airway, which is essential when making a whistle.

To make a tip whistle, drill a hole $1^{1}/_{8}$in (30mm) deep and ¼in (6mm) in diameter into the tip. Make a vertical cut $^{3}/_{16}$in (5mm) deep so it penetrates into the 6mm hole ½in (12mm) from the front of the tip. Make an angled cut starting ½in (12mm) from the vertical cut until it meets with the bottom of the vertical cut to form the airway. Smooth off the sides of the airway. Make a dowel ¼in (6mm) in diameter and $^{5}/_{8}$in (15mm) long from wood or a plastic knitting needle to fit into the mouth of the whistle, and file a flat side along the dowel about $^{1}/_{8}$in (2mm) deep. The flat side can be made with a very gentle taper to divert the air against the shaped airway.

Insert the dowel (reed) into the hole so it emerges at the front edge of the airway, and

Whistle made from an antler tip.

test it to see if it whistles. Move its position until it does. When a clear whistle is achieved, glue the reed in place and finish shaping the mouthpiece. The tone of the whistle will be quite shrill when it is made from an antler tip, which makes it ideal for a dog whistle.

Whistles can also be made on antler tines or the forks of thumb sticks, as long as the porous core (pith) at the bottom of the whistle hole is sealed to prevent the passage of air through it. A small amount of thin superglue dropped into the hole will seal the bottom of the hole, making it airtight.

Measurements for whistles can vary slightly depending on the size of the material available, and changing the diameter and depth of the hole will change the sound of the whistle. It is well worth experimenting and practising whistle making on scrap pieces of antler or wooden shank to gain experience before using a good antler.

If a whistle is fitted to an exhibition stick, ensure that it works because judges will try it out; should it fail the stick will be downgraded.

Using Spacers

Because antler shapes vary so much, finding an antler that perfectly matches with a shank is difficult, so an option regularly used by stickmakers is to fit a spacer between the antler and the shank. The thickness of a spacer can vary considerably so it can be shaped to provide a clean transition between the antler and shank without exposing the pith of the antler or damaging the bark of the shank.

Spacers can be made from acrylic, bone, horn or wood, so always keep a few small offcuts from material cut from handle blanks or other projects. Pre-cut buffalo horn spacers and white camel bone spacers are popular, and are available from some commercial suppliers

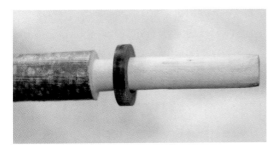

Fitting a spacer on to a dowel.

(*see* Further Information). Several thin spacers of different materials can be used together to form an attractive joint between the handle and shank.

Fitting Caps

Caps can be fitted on to a cut-off tine and a coronet to improve the look of the handle, and they should be made using the same material as a spacer if one is fitted. Because caps are susceptible to knocks they have to be well fitted to reduce the risk of failure. Caps simply glued on to the antler can be easily knocked off if the stick is accidently dropped or falls onto a hard surface, so it is worth spending a little time to make the cap more secure. The joint between the cap and antler has to be a perfect fit to provide as much surface area as possible

for the adhesive to be effective. The following procedure will improve the strength and effectiveness of a cap joint.

Step 1: Make a perfectly flat surface on both the antler and spacer material so that a close-fitting joint can be made.

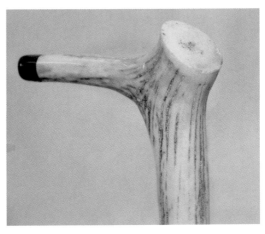

Make a flat surface on the antler.

Step 2: Insert a rust-proof screw with a countersunk head directly into the pith; use some adhesive to strengthen the bond between the screw and antler.

A rust-proof screw is inserted.

Step 3: Drill a shallow hole in the cap to match the diameter of the screw head, making sure the cap fits closely on to the antler.

A shallow hole is drilled in the cap.

The completed cap.

Step 4: Glue the cap on to the antler, filling the hole in the cap with adhesive; secure the cap in place until the adhesive has completely set.

The cap is held in place.

Step 5: Merge the cap and handle together, remove any marks from the cap, and finally polish it.

Making an Antler Stick with a Spacer and Whistle

Step 1: Select a straightened, seasoned shank that will match well with an antler. Use a $5/8$in- (16mm-) diameter turned dowel, and fit it into the straightened shank.

Fitting a dowel.

Step 2: Drill the pith out of the antler using a ⅝in (16mm) flat spade bit. Check that the dowel fits neatly into the antler, making a tight joint. In this example there is a slight gap due to the odd shape of the antler, but a buffalo spacer will be used to make it up.

Checking the joint.

Step 3: Ensure that once the spacer is in place it will make a close joint between the shank and the antler: sometimes a thicker spacer may be required if there is a substantial difference between shank and antler.

Fitting a spacer.

Step 4: To make a whistle on the antler tine, first drill a hole in the tine 1⅛in (30mm) deep and ¼in (6mm) in diameter. Cut out an airway so it just enters into the ¼in (6mm) hole, making the vertical cut ½in (12mm) from the mouth. Make an angled cut to form the airway, smoothing off any rough edges. Seal the bottom of the hole by dripping a few drops of thin superglue into the hole. Make a reed from ¼in- (6mm-) diameter material, and file a flat on to the reed. Insert the reed in the hole, and move it until the whistle works; then glue the reed in place.

Whistle cut into the tine.

Whistle reed in place.

Whistles can be made to fit a range of handles; some makers will fashion a trio of whistles on a three-pronged antler each with a different tone and pitch.

Step 5: When the whistle works and the joint has been checked for fit and alignment, glue the handle on to the shank, keeping the assembly under pressure until the adhesive has completely set.

Hold the antler in position.

Step 6: Dress the joint and spacer so the antler blends perfectly on to the shank, taking care not to damage the bark on the shank. Remove

The completed handle.

all marks on the spacer, and smooth off any rough sections of the antler. Polish the spacer and antler section at the joint. Apply a finish to the shank, and fit a ferrule as and when required.

Making an Antler Thumb Stick

The method of making an antler thumb stick is similar to the technique described above: begin by selecting a straightened shank and make a dowel; drill out a hole in the antler, and check that the shank and antler can be married together. In the example shown the antler is fitted directly on to the shank, so some of the initial steps are not included in the following images.

Step 1: Carefully select a shank and handle, and check that they will merge well together. In this example there is no need to insert a spacer as the antler will fit well on the shank.

Check the fit between shank and antler.

Step 2: Having made a dowel joint, glue the handle on to the shank. Keep the antler handle under pressure while the glue sets to maintain a close-fitting joint between shank and handle.

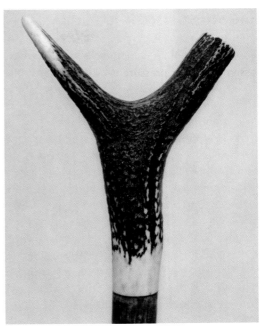

Dress the handle.

Keep the handle under pressure.

Step 3: When the glue has set, dress the antler and joint, ensuring that a smooth transition between antler and shank is achieved.

Step 4: Here, the longer fork has been shortened to match the shorter one to improve the balance of the handle. The stick is finished: there are no caps or spacers fitted, as some people prefer to own a natural-looking antler-handled stick.

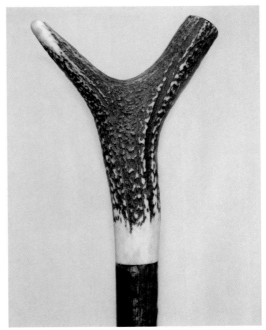

The fork heights are matched.

Cleaning Antler

The natural colour of antler is almost white, like bone. The various colours of the antler when you obtain it is a result of the habitat and environment of the deer, where much of the colouring is dried-on skin, dirt and grime that gets embedded into the antler as the deer forages for food. People's preferences differ: some like the dark antlers, while others prefer them with most of dirt and grime removed, and a few choose a completely clean antler.

Most of the surface muck can be removed by scrubbing the antler with soapy water and a stiff brush. If a mixture of clean antler with a hint of dirt is required a wire brush can be used to remove stubborn dirt, followed by a final cleaning with detergent.

To remove all the dirt from the antler and get back to the natural white colouring you will need to immerse the antler in thin bleach contained in a plastic receptacle for two or three days; when it is clean, place it in clean water for a few hours to neutralize the effect of the bleach. However, a word of caution before cleaning an antler with bleach: remove all the pith by drilling it out, otherwise you will end up with an awful mess in the bottom of your container as the bleach will extrude the pith into the container.

Bending Antler

It has been assumed for a long time that antler cannot be bent, and many methods have been

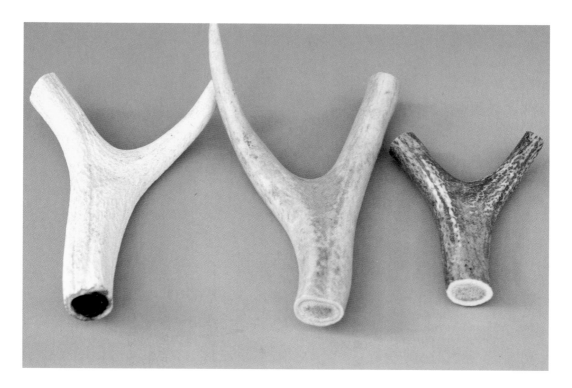

Various colours of antler.

tried without success. However, stickmakers are experimenting with bending antler by immersing it in vinegar for several weeks, and they have had some success. After a period of about six weeks the antler softens in the vinegar sufficiently for it to be bent round a former, and it will set in position when left to dry. It took stick dressers several years to perfect the technique of heating and bending buffalo and sheep's horn, so with practice and the determination typical of stickmakers, it is probable that we will soon be bending and shaping antler, allowing a much wider range of antler handles to be made.

ANTLER BENDING – AN EXPERIMENT

An experiment was carried out to straighten a curved antler and the results were encouraging. The intention was to see if the curved antler could be straightened, thus making it more suitable for a thumb-stick handle that could be held in either hand and in both directions.

The pith was drilled out of the antler to reduce the risk of making a mess in the container.
The antler was then submersed in white (clear) vinegar for a period of seven weeks, it was removed from the vinegar and placed in the press (see Chapter 6) and flattened. A wooden dowel was inserted into the antler to prevent it from collapsing during the squeezing process. The antler was left in the press to allow it to set for four days before it was removed. It was then allowed to dry out naturally.

The two photographs show the antler before and after it was flattened and demonstrate that antler can moved using this method; the next step would be to determine how much an antler tine can be bent.

The antler before bending...

... and after.

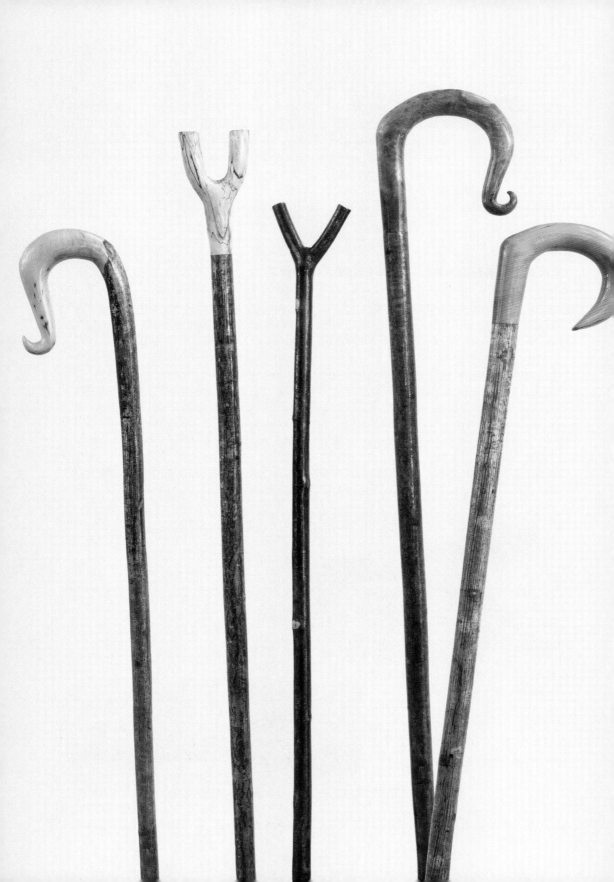

WOODEN HANDLES

Most walking and working sticks and their handles are made using a variety of timbers, and they come in many styles, colours and shapes. They can be categorized into three principal groups: one-piece, two-piece and multi-piece.

One-piece sticks are made from a single piece of wood without any pieces added other than a metal ferrule to protect the tip. Two-piece sticks are made with two different sections; usually a different wood is used for the handle and shank. Multi-piece sticks are less common, as several pieces of timber are used to make the handles; a different timber is generally used for a shank, giving the stick its individual character.

One-Piece Sticks

Crooks, market and walking sticks made in one piece are very popular among stick collectors and discerning users, who like the feel of these light, strong sticks. Some judges will choose a well made one-piece stick over an equally good two-piece stick because one-piece sticks are often regarded as being more difficult to make than a two-piece. The reasons for this opinion are that first, a large section of timber for a handle has to be cut from a tree with a suitable branch attached at the correct angle to make

OPPOSITE: **Wooden handles.**

a shank. Locating such a piece is the first problem; the next is cutting it out of a tree with your folding hand saw, and when it is cut out, you have to carry the heavy block back to your vehicle. Then it must be seasoned for three or more years, ensuring it doesn't crack or split, before you can begin to shape the handle. Finally a serious mistake when working on the handle or shank could render the whole piece to the waste bin, whereas a separate handle or shank can simply be replaced if a mistake is made!

The seasoning time can be reduced by carefully removing equal amounts of timber from both sides of the block, but ensure it does not dry out too quickly by applying a suitable sealant to the wood to reduce the risk of cracks and shakes appearing. Another method of preventing timber drying out too quickly and splitting is to place it in a polythene bag or to wrap it in polythene, which creates a mini-climate for the timber.

NHS Walking Sticks

The most common one-piece sticks are the walking sticks made from chestnut for the National Health Service (NHS): they are the only walking sticks made to comply with a British Standard. These sticks have been heated using steam, and generally have all the bark stripped from them; the round handles are shaped while the shank is still hot. Some sticks are stained while others remain their natural colour; their height varies to accommodate the hundreds of users. Most sticks are fitted with a large rubber ferrule to prevent them from slipping on pavements and other hard surfaces; the sticks are sturdily made, providing safe support for their user.

Natural Thumb Sticks

One of the simplest and yet most popular working sticks are natural one-piece thumb sticks. They are found when a branch forms a fork and two offshoots grow out from the branch. Most offshoots grow unevenly at a different length and thickness, but providing there is sufficient space between the forks for your thumb to sit comfortably, a functional stick can be made.

It is surprisingly difficult to find a naturally grown thumb stick with a pair of perfectly matching forks and a parallel shank. Most natural thumb-stick shanks are larger at the bottom of the shank than the top due to the way the branch grows. Try to avoid cutting a shank where the lower end is considerably larger and heavier than the top, as it will feel unbalanced and will be awkward to use. The most sought-after natural thumb sticks are those with a pair of perfectly matching forks and a straight parallel shank. A stick with these features will often be placed higher in a competition than a two-piece version because of the time taken to locate it, and the fact that nature has provided a perfect specimen, which is quite a rare find.

When the shank is fully seasoned, straighten it as described in the previous chapter, cut the forks to the same height, and dress the tips; the edges of the tips can be rounded or left flat. Finally remove any scratches or saw marks. Carefully smooth off the bark and any stubs left from offshoots, cut the stick to length and fit a ferrule on the bottom, and apply a suitable outdoor finish.

Occasionally the bark has to be stripped from the shank if it has been badly damaged or marked while growing; this is an acceptable practice in a plain thumb-stick class, but it might not be deemed a natural stick by some show judges if the class is for naturally grown sticks. This is a subtle but important difference when exhibiting a stick.

One-Piece Knob Sticks

There are a number of established shapes for knob-handled sticks which have been used for

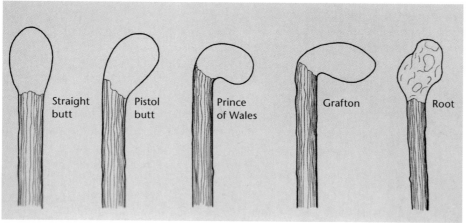

Straight butt | Pistol butt | Prince of Wales | Grafton | Root

Traditional knob-stick shapes.

years, but there is no right or wrong shape for a knob stick, the main requirement being that the handle is comfortable to hold. Most knob sticks are made for walking, and the height of the stick is usually similar to a traditional walking stick, which is about 36in (915mm), but because people prefer longer or shorter lengths it is advisable to fit a ferrule when the stick is sold or given to its new owner.

Making a Knob Stick

To make a one-piece knob stick you will need a decent shank with a section of a branch about 3in (75mm) in diameter on top of the shank. Remember that a 3in piece of wood will require two or three years to season, so making a knob stick is a longer-term project.

A knob-stick block.

Shaping the seasoned block is done using rasps and abrasives, always remembering to avoid making deep marks and cuts in the surface with coarse rasps. With a belt or disc sanding machine a block can be roughly fashioned quite quickly on a coarse belt or disc, and then carefully finished by hand. It is important

to achieve a smooth knob that fits comfortably into the hand of the user. The seasoned shank is straightened and a ferrule fitted, and a finish is applied to complete the stick. The illustration shows a simple knob stick that can be made quickly from an unexceptional block.

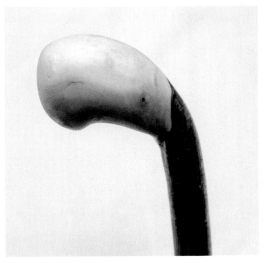

A simple knob stick.

Making a One-Piece Leg Cleek

When making a one-piece leg cleek it is important to be patient and avoid cutting too much material off the block at any one time. Note that the block used here was cut longer than required to allow for some splitting and cracking during the seasoning period.

Step 1: Cut excess timber from both sides of the block to form two flat sides that align with the shank. The waste can be removed using a hand saw or a portable electric planer. Using a planer gives greater control as smaller amounts of wood are removed with each pass – although there is more mess to clear up.

Step 2: Draw the shape of your selected handle on one of the flat sides, ensuring that the shank blends into the handle, resulting in clean inside and outside lines between the shank and the handle. A Perspex former is ideal for marking out the block: because it is transparent, the lines of the handle and the shape of the shank can be seen through the former, making it easier to align the handle with the shank.

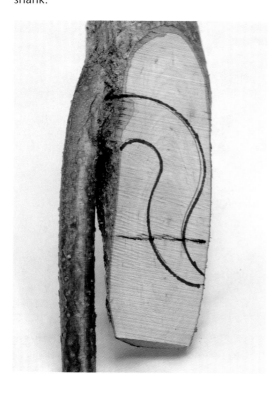

The shape is drawn on the flattened side.

Step 3: Cut out the shape of the handle; begin carefully to remove surplus wood from the inside and outside lines using a coping or jigsaw, ensuring that a smooth transition is

maintained between the handle and shank. A bandsaw with a narrow blade can be used with care if available. Leave a little spare timber on each flat side and along the inside and outside lines to allow for any error that may occur during the shaping process.

The shape is cut out.

Step 4: Begin shaping the handle using rasps to remove the excess material; ensure that the handle and shank blend well together, making a seamless connection. Avoid using coarse rasps too close to the inside and outside lines when shaping the handle as they may create deep marks which are difficult to remove. Complete shaping the handle using abrasives in sequence – for example 80 grit, then 100 grit to 120 to 150 and so on, until all scratches and marks are removed from the timber.

Step 5: When most of the shaping is complete, straighten the shank ensuring it remains aligned with the handle. Be aware that it is not

Shaping is progressing.

Step 6: Seal the timber with sanding sealer, and when it is dry, apply a finish of your choice using several thin coats. When the finish has completely dried, check it for any minor defects; if satisfied, give the stick a final polish. Fit a ferrule when the length of the stick is decided.

The finished stick.

always possible to remove severe bends that are positioned close to the heel due to the grain formation of the wood, so never force the shank and risk damaging the stick at this stage. When satisfied that the handle and shank are aligned, finish the handle and remove any defects from the shank. Check the measurements of the handle, ensuring that they are within allowable tolerances; in this instance one old penny and one halfpenny are used.

Checking the measurements.

Other One-Piece Handles

One-piece sticks can be made by digging out a root with a shank growing directly off the root. Blackthorn sticks are often made using this method. Hedgerows that have been cut and laid for a few years can produce interesting handle-sized branches, and often a horizontally laid branch will have strong, straight offshoots rising vertically up through the hedge, which make excellent cross-handled sticks.

If you decide to cut sticks from hedgerows, be sure to obtain permission from the owner, and ensure you do not leave gaps that will affect the integrity of the hedge.

Because of the grain configuration in one-piece handles they make strong, light sticks that will withstand a lot of outdoor use, making them a popular choice amongst people interested in outdoor country pursuits.

Market Sticks

A market stick is shorter than a crook and longer than a standard walking stick; typically its height is measured from the ground to the bottom of the user's chest bone, which is about 44in (1,120mm) for an average-sized person. It is thought that this style of stick originated from drovers who made a living herding livestock around the country. The drover would cut a stick from a hedgerow or bush as an aid to assist him when driving his animals over many miles of rough terrain. When the drover rested, and while sitting and talking with his colleagues, he would whittle away at his stick to improve its look and feel. Like the present time, some drovers were talented and could fashion a beautiful and functional stick from a simple branch. When he reached the end of the journey he would probably sell or exchange his stick with the farmers or stockmen who used this type of stick when they attended livestock and cattle markets.

A market stick was often regarded as the farmer's 'best' stick: it was his showpiece on those important days when he could make or spend a considerable amount of money, depending on whether he was selling or buying.

The nose of a market stick is normally turned in, but there is no reason why it cannot be turned out. However, it is important that the gape or mouth of the stick will slip over the wrist and hang comfortably on the lower arm of the user so that both hands are free for the farmer to negotiate his deal at the market.

Tradition aside, this style of stick remains popular because it is comfortable to use, lean on and walk with, and the handles can be used to pull down those hard-to-reach brambles and sloes.

Making a Two-Piece Market Stick

The handle and shank in the following example are made from different pieces of timber, the shank from dark hazel and the handle from a piece of burr elm.

Step 1: Draw the outline shape of the handle on to a piece of timber, and cut out the desired shape. The blank in the example was cut out using a bandsaw. Select a suitable seasoned and straightened shank that will nicely match the handle.

Cut a blank to shape.

Step 2: Begin shaping the handle using rasps, taking care not to create deep marks in the wood. Work from both sides of the blank so the handle is evenly shaped; leave a small amount of surplus wood on the handle until it is joined to the shank. Drawing a centre line around the blank helps to maintain an even shape.

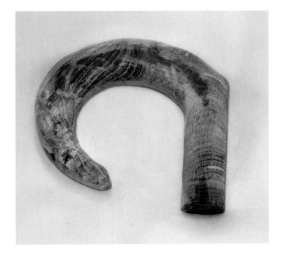

Begin shaping the handle.

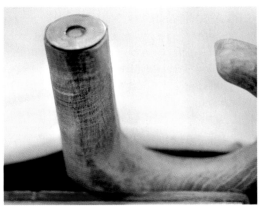

Preparing to drill the handle.

Step 3: When the handle is roughly shaped, mark out the best position to insert a piece of $^7/_8$in- (8mm-) diameter studding for the joint. A 1in- (25mm-) diameter washer with an $^7/_8$in (8mm) hole is ideal for marking the position of the hole. Make sure that the surface of the handle section to be jointed is perfectly flat so a close joint is made. (*The joint can be cut at an angle if preferred, providing the surface is flat.*) Drill a $^7/_8$in- (8mm-) diameter hole to a depth of about 2in (50mm) into the handle, making sure it is perfectly true so the shank and handle will be accurately aligned.

Step 4: Cut a piece of $^7/_8$in (8mm) mild steel threaded studding about 5in (125mm) long, and, using a suitable adhesive, glue it into the handle, ensuring it is perfectly aligned with the inside line of the handle. Remove any surplus glue, especially from the flat surface so it does not impede making a close joint.

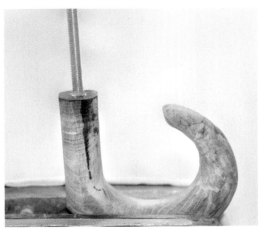

The studding is glued into the handle.

Step 5: Check that your chosen shank is a good match with the handle. Using a washer, mark the best position to drill a $^7/_8$in (8mm) hole in the shank. Drill the hole to a depth of 3in (75mm), again making sure the hole is correctly aligned with the handle. Ensure the end of the shank is flat so it fits closely to the handle, and wrap some masking tape around the shank to protect it from excess glue, and so an identification mark can be made on the shank. Fit the handle and shank together to test the alignment, and with a pencil, mark with a line the best position on both the shank (tape) and handle. When satisfied that the alignment and the joint are good, glue the shank on to the handle.

Step 6: When the glue has set, complete shaping the handle so that it merges perfectly on to the shank, ensuring that the inside line of the handle and shank are aligned. Remove all marks from the handle using abrasives in sequence from coarse to fine, taking care not to damage the bark on the shank.

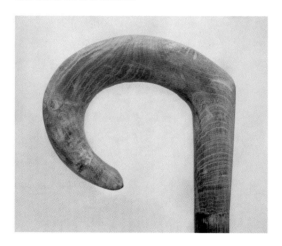

The handle is fitted on to the shank.

Step 7: Complete the shank, remove any loose bark, and smooth off any stubs left from offshoots. Check that the shank is straight and is aligned with the handle. If the shank is bent, remove the bends. Providing the length of the shank is known, fit a ferrule; otherwise leave a longer shank that can be shortened later. With the shank and handle complete, apply sanding sealer to both. Additional coats may be applied if necessary.

Step 8: When the sealer is completely dry,

smooth off all surfaces with a fine abrasive; wire wool rated 0000 or burnishing cream are suitable as a preparation for applying a final finish. The stick in the example is finished with several coats of melamine gloss lacquer.

The completed stick.

The techniques used to make both the block and market stick featured can be adapted to make most types and styles of wooden-handled sticks.

Multi-Piece Wooden Sticks

Some stickmakers enjoy making multi-piece sticks using a mixture of timbers. The styles, shapes and sizes of these sticks vary considerably, and the imagination, talent and skill of some stickmakers is incredible, with many wonderful examples on display at agricultural shows and country fairs. Fitting caps and spacers to thumb-stick handles using a contrasting coloured timber is a simple example of multi-piece sticks. Laminated handles using thin layers of different timbers glued together make interesting and unique sticks. A few stickmakers carve images using different timbers to enhance particular features of a carved handle. Handles are also made using a mixture of wooden rings glued together on a shaped metal rod. It is difficult to cut the number of accurately angled joints required to make a curved handle using this method, but the results can be impressive when done by a skilled craftsperson.

Crooks

There are several traditional patterns of crook handle available for crooks, as mentioned in Chapter 1. Knowledgeable stick collectors amass well made wooden-handled crooks, especially when the handle represents an old-fashioned shape that is seldom made nowadays. The shape of the modern crook has developed over several decades as a result of feedback from shepherds who require a light, strong crook that will slip over the neck of their sheep and hold it without causing the animal any harm. The typical crook length varies between 44in (1,220mm) and 52in (1,320mm), depending on the height of the shepherd. One suggested width of the mouth of a crook is four fingers, which can equate to between 3in and 3¾in (75mm and 95mm), depending on the size of the hand. Sheep sizes vary according to their breed, and shepherds tend to choose crooks to use with a particular breed.

When a shepherd uses his crook to catch and hold a sheep he holds it with the handle furthest from his hand, about a third of the way down from the ferrule. A handle that is too heavy will make the stick unbalanced, so it becomes a tiresome tool to work with. A parallel shank on a crook helps to maintain the balance of the stick during use, while a severely tapered shank may make the stick top heavy when it is being used to catch and hold a sheep.

A crook should have a strong ferrule fitted on the tip so it can be plunged into the ground; it should also have a turned-out nose so the shepherd can hang a lamp or his jacket from it while attending to the sheep. The ferrule should be recessed into the shank to give a smooth surface between it and the shank, because the sharp edge of a ferrule protruding from a shank can cause serious injury if the crook is pulled through the shepherd's hand by a strong sheep.

Wooden crook handles are not as strong as those made from horn, and are seldom used in a working crook, but they are often used to make an attractive walking stick or as an exhibition piece.

Thumb Sticks

As mentioned earlier, thumb sticks are one of the most popular types of stick, and using separate pieces of wood to make a handle increases the scope of handles that can be made. The most common shape is probably the lyre, but there are many variations of handle in regular use. The most important factor when making a thumb-stick handle is that the thumb can fit comfortably into the bottom of the handle when in use, and ideally it can be used by either hand and in both directions, a point to be aware of if you intend to enter stickmaking competitions.

A thumb-stick handle must be made so it allows the thumb to be released in the event of a trip or fall; there have been instances where a person's thumb became trapped in a small hole in the handle when the user slipped or tripped, resulting in a broken thumb.

Thumb sticks are often used to lean on, and

the height of a thumb stick is often measured so it fits under the armpit, allowing the user to rest for while during a long walk. A typical length for a thumb stick is 50in (1,270mm), but this will vary considerably from person to person. Tall thumb sticks are sometimes requested for use as rifle and camera rests, but they require a wider fork than normal to accommodate a gun or camera lens.

Walking Sticks

People often select a short stick to provide them with support when walking. It is important that these sticks are sturdy, comfortable to hold, and have a well fitted ferrule to give the user confidence. A lady's hand is generally smaller than a man's, and therefore a lady will prefer a smaller handle that fits to her hand. A large man may request a more substantial handle fitted to a heavier shank to give him adequate support – so again, there is no fixed size or length for a walking stick. The typical height for a lady's stick is about 34in (865mm), and 36in (915mm) for a man's. It is crucial that the user feels and is comfortable and confident with a walking stick, so allow a potential owner to try it out and have any adjustments made before taking it away. Have a selection of rubber ferrules on hand, as customers often request one to be fitted on their chosen walking stick.

There are several styles of handle that can be made for short sticks, and two of the most popular are the simple cross-head and the round handle; others in regular use are the crutch, derby, cardigan and knob handles, all of which will give support. Avoid making long wooden handles on walking sticks because people tend to grip the end of a handle, and this puts a lot of pressure on the joint, which may cause it to fail.

When making a stick for other people, explain to them that when in use, the most weight should be applied directly on top of the shank, as this is the strongest part of the handle and stick. Sometimes a stick can be held in the reverse direction so the person's arm is directly above the shank, which gives maximum support.

Hikers may use a staff when walking long distances, often over rough and undulating terrain. A staff is generally considerably longer than a walking stick so it provides support when the hiker is ascending or descending steep hills. It needs to be strong and fairly light so it isn't too cumbersome for the user on long journeys. Some users request that a lanyard is attached to the staff, which can be secured to a wrist to prevent the staff from been accidently lost in the event of a trip or fall. Lanyards can be obtained from some commercial suppliers (see Further Information).

Turned Handles and Canes

Turned handles attract considerable attention from the public and make a nice display feature. Wooden handles can be turned on a lathe using up small pieces of timber that might otherwise be scrapped. Most timbers can be turned successfully, and the shapes that can be made are endless. Different types of wood can be glued together, and when two contrasting colours are used together and turned the result can be very effective.

To turn a handle, drill a $7/8$in (8mm) hole into the wood and glue in a length of 8mm threaded rod. When the glue has set, use the rod to hold the handle in the lathe during the turning, which keeps the rod in a central position. A neat recess can be turned to fit an engraved or plain collar; this gives the handle and stick more character, and allows the handle to be easily fitted to a natural shank or a turned

Turned handles.

shank. If the lathe bed is too short, two sections can be turned and a brass connector used to join the two pieces together.

Making Templates

If it is intended to make several sticks it is well worth making templates of your favourite shapes so that accurate copies can be made in the future. Plywood or sheets of clear plastic can be used for the template, though a clear template is best, as the lie of the grain in the wood can be seen through the plastic, and the best position found before marking out the handle ready for cutting and shaping.

Some suppliers have excellent pre-shaped wooden blanks for sale, and it is worth considering buying a selection to use as a pattern for your templates, or to use them to make handles for your own sticks. Handles can be made from most woods, although some are better than others, depending on the type of handle you intend to make. A walking or working stick requires a handle and shank that will withstand the arduous conditions it is exposed to while in regular use. Exhibition sticks are sometimes made from wood that is unsuitable for the onerous duties of a working stick, and a conscientious stickmaker should always advise a potential customer of the limitations of an exhibition stick made from these timbers.

A lot of timber is supplied in planks, which are ideal for making stick handles, especially if the thickness is around 1¼in (30mm). There is a wide range of native and exotic woods from overseas to choose from, each with its own grain and colour configurations.

Planked timber is useful because there is little waste; often several handles can be made from a plank of wood. Planks can be cut with a bandsaw, a coping saw or a jigsaw, and the handle shaped with carving tools or rasps and later smoothed off with abrasives, before completing it with your favourite finishing product.

A clean, strong joint between the handle and shank is important, and anyone starting out to make sticks will require a drill to make a hole in the handle for a dowel or rod. A traditional style of brace and bit or a hand-operated drill can be used to drill a hole in the handle, though nowadays most people own a battery- or mains-powered drill that is ideal for this job.

CHAPTER FIVE

BUFFALO HORN HANDLES

Most buffalo horn is imported from India and China, and yet it is easier to obtain than British-reared sheep's horn. The solid tips of buffalo horn are used for stickmaking, and they are available in lengths exceeding 18in (460mm), which is more than sufficient for a fully decorated crook, making them a popular choice with stickmakers. Short, heavy sections of horn can also be obtained, which are ideal for making cardigan or half-head handles. Pieces of horn can also be purchased in round and flat sections, which are useful for making caps, spacers and long ferrules.

Pre-shaped handles are available, ranging from thumb sticks, riding crops and derby handles, and these need only a small amount of work to finish them to an acceptable standard. Two types of partly bent handles large enough to make market sticks and shepherd crooks are also available, although they do require some work to complete them – for example, the nose has to be turned out to make a crook, and it needs to be turned in a little for a market stick. The advantage of these pre-shaped handles is that they enable people who don't have horn-bending equipment to make their own handle from buffalo horn.

Please be aware that you should not enter pre-shaped handles in stickmaking competitions, as the rules require that a stick must be made completely by the competitor. Experienced judges can identify some of the most common pre-shaped handles, and they will place them at the back of the rack without making any comment to avoid conflict with the contestant; showing is based very much on trust and the honesty of the competitors, who are responsible for any sticks they enter in competitions.

Selecting Horn

Over many decades stickmakers have improved the technique of working and shaping buffalo horn, and today we can use their knowledge and experience to manipulate the horn with much less difficulty than they encountered. As a result, buffalo horn has become popular, and a lot of is bought on-line; selecting the most suitable horn is therefore a little uncertain, so choose a reputable supplier who will listen to your requirements and will try to supply you with a piece that meets your specifications. Suppliers often grade the horn, and while some lower graded horns will make handles, it is advisable to select the better grades if you intend to make a top quality handle, as they should have fewer flaws and blemishes.

Be sure to order a horn that is large enough to make your handle – and the width is just as important as the length, because it must be wide enough to fit on to the shank you plan to use. If possible, visit a supplier so you can exam-

OPPOSITE: **Buffalo horn sticks.**

ine the horn before buying to avoid disappoint-ment; otherwise use a reputable supplier, who will do their best to supply a horn that meets your requirements.

Coloured Buffalo Horn

Most buffalo horn is coloured black; occasion-ally some horns have streaks of colour runn-ing within the horn, which gives it added charac-ter. Coloured horn makes stunning handles, but is in very short supply and demands premium prices when it is available. Coloured horns are also bought by clothing manufacturers, who use them to make buttons and other accessories on exclusive clothes. Very occasionally coloured horn is available from commercial suppliers (*see* Further Information).

Horn Sizes

After deciding on the type of handle you intend to make, look for a piece of horn taking quality, length and thickness into consideration. The following list gives examples of the minimum length of horn required to make a particular style of handle, though it is advisable to buy longer pieces because sometimes the tip may be damaged or unsuitable.

- A lady's walking stick will require a horn of 12in (305mm) for a nose-in handle
- A market stick will require a horn of 13in (330mm) for a nose-in handle
- A market stick will require a horn of 15in (380mm) for a nose-out handle
- A plain crook will require a horn in excess of 16in (410mm) for a turned-out nose
- A carved handle will require a larger piece of horn than a plain handle, especially if it is intended to carve an object on to the nose section

Tools and Equipment

In order to successfully work and shape buffalo horn it will be necessary to obtain a range of tools and equipment for use with horn. Engi-neering tools are more suitable than wood-working equipment as they are designed to cut hard materials, and good quality engineer-ing tools such as drills and files will cope easily with buffalo and other horn. A few specialized tools are introduced in this chapter for work-ing and shaping buffalo horn, but stickmakers are ingenious people and will make or adapt tools for their own use based on these familiar patterns.

Cutting the Horn

Buffalo horn is much harder than some timbers so you need a saw with a suitable blade to cut off surplus horn. Hacksaws and coping saws can be used, but the best option is a band-saw fitted with an appropriate blade; a narrow blade will cut sharp curves and corners, making it ideal for cutting handles, formers and even aluminium bulking blocks. It will quickly cut off surplus buffalo horn, though after a time the work will blunt the blade and it will be unsuit-able for cutting timber; it is advisable to keep a blade specifically for this job and not use it to cut other materials.

Before cutting off surplus horn, draw the outline dimensions of the handle on to the horn, keeping the shape equally spaced along the centre line of the horn as far as possible. This reduces the chances of hitting the centre core of the horn during the later stages of finishing the handle. Mark the approximate position of the heel on the horn, using the base of the neck as the datum reference. If a square heel is to be made, this needs to be marked on the horn so the horn is cut to shape correctly. If a round heel is required, simply draw a curved line following the contour of the horn. Make sufficient allowance when marking out the horn if a figure, such as an animal or thistle, is to be carved on to the horn.

Cutting off surplus horn will make the bending and shaping process easier, but be careful not to remove too much horn at this early stage, as it is possible to remove more later on in the procedure. Keep the larger offcuts as they will make spacers or caps in the future. The horn in the image has been cut to make a square heel on the handle and is used in the next sequence.

Surplus horn is removed.

Bending Horn

Heating the Horn

Buffalo horn has to be heated in order to bend it, and there are two methods of heating horn that are used: wet and dry heat. In wet heat, the horn is placed in boiling water; in dry heat, a gas flame or an electric hot-air gun is used. Gas torches and old-fashioned blowlamps can be used with care to heat the horn, but are seldom used because of the severity of the heat they generate; the horn can be protected by wrapping it with baking foil. Electric hot-air guns are mostly used to heat horn; the best ones have variable heat control which

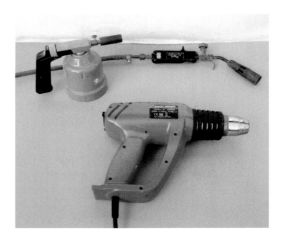

Gas torches and hot-air gun.

is an advantage, especially when turning noses. The guns are available from most DIY and hardware shops for about £30 (at the time of writing).

A large receptacle is required so a horn can be fully submerged in water and then heated on gas or electric rings; another option is to use an electric urn – the type often used in kitchens and cafes is ideal. It is recommended that boiling horns is done outside the house as it does cause an unpleasant smell, which can take some time to disperse.

A horn ready for boiling in a jam pan.

Boiling the Horn

Boiling horn in water is the best method of heating it prior to bending; it keeps the horn moist and will not burn the horn. Place the horn into a container of boiling water for 30 to 40 minutes depending on its size, making sure the container does not run out of water.

While the horn is boiling, prepare the former and clamps in readiness for the bending procedure. Have a hot-air gun to hand to maintain heat in the horn, and have some blocks and wedges ready to align the horn as the bending progresses.

It is possible to heat a horn using a hot-air gun or naked flame (dry heat) if boiling is not possible, but take care not to burn it. Keep the gun or flame moving over the surface of the horn at all times, and allow sufficient time for the heat to penetrate deep into the horn. If the heat is not allowed to penetrate into the horn it is likely to crack if too much pressure is applied during the bending process.

Bending Jigs and Formers

Formers
Bending horn to a particular shape is best done using a former that can be made from hardwood, tufnol, aluminium or steel. Metal formers will last longer than wood or tufnol and are worth making if you intend to make several handles. If you just want to make a few handles, hardwood or tufnol formers can be used; they will burn or crack if used frequently, but new ones can be made quickly with a jig- or bandsaw to replace them. Formers must be fastened to the bending jig firmly in order to withstand the forces when bending horn around them.

Bending Jigs
The baseplate of the bending jig should be made from a piece of flat steel plate so it will withstand the heat and pressure applied during the bending and shaping procedure, and so it can be held securely in a vice or on a workbench. A clamp to hold the handle neck tightly in position is welded on to one side of the baseplate. Three pairs of holes are drilled in the baseplate so the former may be located in three separate positions for different sizes of horn. A further series of holes are drilled around the edge so that anchor points can be bolted on to the baseplate; the anchor points are used with clamps to pull the horn on to the former. The anchor points can be positioned in different locations on the baseplate, which is important as the horn is bent round the former and the clamps are repositioned.

Bending jigs and aluminium formers.

Two bending jigs are shown in the photo: the smaller red one is 10sq in (64.5sq cm) and is used most; the larger plain steel jig is 12sq in (77sq cm) and is designed to take strong threaded rods that hold the horn in position, reducing the number of clamps needed. The rods can be dropped into any of the holes drilled in a semi-circle around the former. The formers and anchor bars will fit on both of the jigs featured.

The Bending Process

Several strong clamps are required to pull the hot horn round the former and hold it firmly in place until it cools and sets in position. The horn must be kept very hot during the bending process, and this is achieved by using a hot-air gun to maintain the heat in the section of horn being bent. Whenever you halt the bending sequence it is important to clamp the horn tightly against the former until it cools and sets; if the horn is released too soon it will try to revert back to its original shape and this will cause it to crack on the inside line, completely spoiling the handle. As explained above, the larger of the two jigs is equipped to hold the horn in position using threaded bolts rather than clamps.

Finishing a Horn Handle

With the handle jointed on to the shank, the handle can be finished. Use fine files and abrasives to merge the handle with the shank, and remove any defects and marks from the handle. Use fine wire wool with 'T Cut' scratch remover to finish the horn. Do not apply this method on a stripped shank as the paste may cause stain marks on the wood; only use dry abrasives on stripped timber.

Buffalo horn can be finished to a very high gloss by buffing and polishing the horn using rotary mops and polishing compound. Purpose-made polishing machines using rotary mops are available and are the best choice for this work; an alternative method is to fit adaptors on to a standard grinding machine to hold the rotary mops, however take care, as some grinder motors are not rated for this type of application. The surface of buffalo horn can be maintained if it is treated with a quality polish: car polishes work well.

If you intend to varnish or lacquer the handle avoid polishing it too much, as these products do not adhere successfully to a highly polished surface; instead prepare a smooth, clean matt surface so the finish will adhere to it.

Cut the shank to length and fit a ferrule, ensuring a good joint is made.

Finally apply a finish of your choice to the shank; it may require several coats to complete the job.

Making a Nose-in Buffalo Market Stick

The following guide describes the principal steps required when making a nose-in market stick from buffalo horn.

Step 1: Select a suitable horn to make the handle; mark the outline shape of the handle on the horn, and cut off any surplus horn. In the example, most of the horn was used as the size was suitable for a market stick, though a section was removed from the neck to help form a square heel. The cut horn used in this sequence is shown in the image used in the earlier section 'Cutting the Horn'.

Step 2: Submerge the horn in boiling water for 35 to 40 minutes. While the horn is boiling, prepare a bending jig and attach a bending former. Lay out sufficient clamps and have a hot-air gun to hand, ready for the bending process. It is useful to have some non-slip blocks available to prevent the clamps from slipping on the horn. Use tongs or gloves to remove the hot horn from the boiling water, and fasten it firmly in position on the bending jig.

Step 3: With the hot horn securely fastened on the jig, use a strong clamp to begin pulling the first bend on to the former. Always maintain heat on the inside line of the horn using the hot-air gun. Note the use of an anchor bar made from angle iron bolted on to the jig, and the non-slip wooden block to prevent the clamp from slipping off the horn during the bending process.

Pulling the first bend.

Step 4: Keep the first bend held tightly in position against the former, and use a second clamp to pull the next section of the horn on to the former. Release the first clamp as soon as the second clamp begins to move the horn. Keep heating the horn on the inside line with the hot-air gun at all times during the bending sequence. Again, note the non-slip wooden

Pulling the second bend.

blocks used to prevent the clamps from slipping off the horn.

Complete bending the crown section of the handle, ensuring that the bent sections of horn are always held tightly against the former. Do not allow the horn to move off the former while it is hot or it may crack on the inside line.

Step 5: With the crown section complete, begin pulling the nose round the former. Keep heating the inside line of the nose with the hot-air gun. A clamp is positioned across the jig to pull the nose on to the former; in the illustration the clamp is held against the heel section of the horn, as this enables the nose to be pulled on to the former. Note that another clamp is used to keep the crown of the horn held against the former while the nose is pulled round. Complete pulling the horn round the former to make a nose-in shaped handle.

Pulling the nose section.

Step 6: Use a tapered wedge to centralize the nose if required (sometimes a screwdriver is suitable); a second clamp is used to keep the crown and nose held against the base of the jig. When the bending sequence is complete, allow the horn to cool down; set it in position before removing it from the jig.

Completing the bending sequence.

Step 7: Begin dressing the horn using files and rasps. Remove the waste equally from both sides of the horn to keep it balanced, using the inside line as a datum for the shape of the handle. Note that a decent square heel has been formed by cutting the horn as shown in the image in the earlier section 'Cutting the Horn' and holding it tightly against the former during the bending sequence.

Beginning to dress the horn.

Step 8: Continue dressing the horn, being careful to avoid making deep marks with the coarser files. Use finer files and abrasives to reduce and shape the horn. Using a 1in × $^7/_8$in (25 × 8mm) diameter washer, mark the position for the studding hole, and draw a circle on to

the horn as a guide for the finished diameter of the handle.

Dressing continues.

Step 9: Before completing the final shaping and dressing of the handle, it must be glued to the shank. This allows the handle and shank to be accurately married together, and any adjustments can be made before the final finishing sequence. A smooth transition between the handle and shank is important if the stick is to look well finished. A section of $^7/_8$in (8mm) threaded studding is used for the joint. A bone spacer is fitted between the handle and shank to give the stick added character. The inside line of the handle is aligned with the shank when joining a handle to a shank.

Glueing the handle to the shank.

Step 10: Allow the adhesive time to set fully before finally dressing the handle and shank. Take great care not to damage the bark on the shank when dressing the horn: wrap masking tape or thin plastic (from a milk container) around the shank to reduce this risk of damage. Use very smooth files to carefully make a smooth joint between the handle and shank, ensuring all traces of glue have been removed. Use abrasives in sequence (coarse to fine) to remove any scratch marks from the horn and shank. Use a paste or liquid abrasive with fine wire wool to complete the dressing of the horn: this will leave a smooth matt finish.

When satisfied that there are no defects, buff the horn using rotary mops to make a polished surface on the horn and spacer. The handle and spacer dressing is then complete, and a close joint has been made between the shank, spacer and handle.

Fit a ferrule to the tip of the shank if the length of the stick is known. The ferrule may be fitted later to suit the new owner.

Step 11: To complete the stick, apply sanding sealer to the shank, followed by several coats of melamine. Use wax to protect the polished horn.

Turning a Nose-out Handle

If a turned-out nose is required on buffalo horn, such as is used on crook-shaped handles, a longer length of horn is required. The horn used to make the previous market stick is too short for a turned-out nose.

Use the same bending jig with a crook-shaped former attached; a longer horn can be bent and shaped using the same method as described for the market stick handle until the nose section is reached.

Step 1: Refer to the image used in the earlier section 'Bending Jigs'. The series of holes drilled close to the bending former is used for turning noses. Fasten a $^3/_8$in (10mm) bolt on to the baseplate in a hole that suits the position of the horn, so the point of the bend fits tightly against the bolt. Re-fix the neck and crown of the handle on the jig to prevent it from moving during the nose-bending sequence; the horn must be fastened tightly on the jig to prevent any such movement.

Use a hot-air gun to heat the section of horn to be bent: concentrate most of the heat on the inside line at the point of the bend – a piece of flat steel or steel ruler may be used to deflect the heat directly on to the point of the bend. Anchor a clamp in a suitable position on the

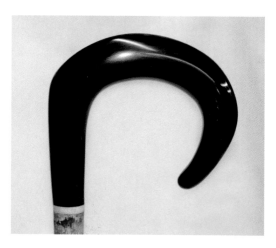

The finished stick.

Turning the first bend of the turned-out nose.

jig, and use it to pull the nose round the bolt. Do not overheat the horn: keep the horn under slight pressure with the clamp, and as soon as it begins to turn, stop the heat and make the first bend. Allow the horn to cool for a while until it stays in this position, and then release the pressure on the clamp. Note that a second clamp is used to keep the horn held tightly against the baseplate to keep it aligned during the bending sequence.

Step 2: The position of the clamp will have to be changed a few times during the bending sequence so the horn can be turned completely round the bolt. The hot horn can be held in place with a second clamp if space permits; if using only one clamp, allow the horn to cool sufficiently between each sequence so that it doesn't move when the clamp is released and repositioned, otherwise it is likely to crack on the inside of the bend.

Throughout the bending sequence ensure the nose is aligned with the handle and heel by using wedges to keep the horn in line.

Finally allow the horn to cool completely and set, before completing the final dressing.

During the nose-bending sequence the horn

The turned-out nose.

may move a little. If this occurs the horn can be reheated and pulled against the former to improve the shape. It is important that the horn is held securely in place when applying heat as it will try to revert to its original shape when heated and cracks may appear in it, especially along the inside line if it is not held tightly in place.

A golden rule: Always keep a hot horn clamped tightly: never allow it to open.

SHEEP AND COW HORN HANDLES

Handles from sheep and cow horn are the most complex and difficult to make, for several reasons: suitable horn is difficult to obtain, specialized tools and equipment are required to manipulate the horn, and working the horn requires a considerable amount of patience, time and experience, which can only be obtained with practice. It is advisable to learn the craft of manoeuvring the material with some 'practice' horns before using expensive and scarce ones; the best option is to have lessons with an experienced dresser if possible.

The following guide describes the type of equipment required to dress cow and sheep horn, and some of the methods used to shape and manipulate the horn. Stickmakers familiar with dressing horns use equipment and methods similar to those described here, but may have modified and customized their own equipment and techniques to achieve the same end result.

The supply of good quality sheep and cow horn suitable for stickmaking has become much reduced over the years as a result of modern farming and breeding practices, and also because of the strict regulations that control the movement of cattle and their parts. Horn is

available from some commercial suppliers (*see* Further Information); it can also be bought on the internet – though take care if buying over the internet as the horn is sometimes of poor quality and unsuitable for making handles. Like buffalo horn, it is best seen before buying to avoid disappointment, but if this is impossible use reputable suppliers.

Selecting Horn

Begin by selecting a suitable length of horn for the handle; it is also very important to choose a horn with thick walls that will withstand being bulked (squeezed) without the horn collapsing. Some rams' horns are very large, making them difficult to work; however, some of the large sections will make excellent thumb-stick handles, spacers, caps and ferrules, so never throw away any heavy sections of horn.

The illustration shows four sheep horns: the walls of the two horns on the left are too thin to be of use to stickmakers, while the black horn has thick walls but a large hollow section, making it more difficult to bulk – although with care it will make a fine handle. The horn on the right is the best option as it has thick walls and a smaller hollow section so it will bulk up nicely. It does have a deep concave side that will have to be removed before starting the bulking process, or a crease will form in the horn when it is squeezed in the bulking press.

OPPOSITE: **Rams' horns.**

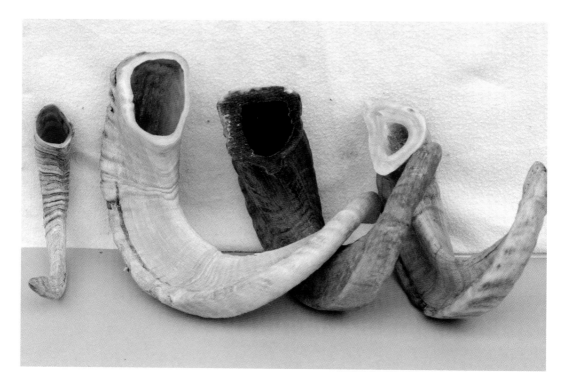

Various thicknesses of horn.

Sheep Horn

Sheep horn colours vary considerably depending on the breed, and range from black to a plain off-white shade. Sheep butt each other, especially during the breeding season, and when they clash their horns can be bruised, causing the formation of blood blisters within the horn. Sometimes a blood colour is visible in the horn warning that a blister may have formed just under the surface; sometimes when dressing a horn a blister can suddenly appear without warning, and a large blister can ruin what was potentially a good horn because it creates a void in the horn that cannot be hidden. If a horn is held close to a bright light a blood blister can sometimes be seen inside the horn, giving the maker some warning of its existence.

Cow Horn

Because of rigorous regulations good quality British cow horns are extremely difficult to obtain. Some cow horns suitable for stick-making are imported, and are available from some of the same suppliers of sheep's horn, or from the internet. Like sheep, some breeds of cow produce beautifully coloured horns that make fantastic handles and are sought after by discerning collectors.

Cow horn is mostly hollow apart from the tip section, and the walls are often quite thin, making the horn difficult to bulk up, so choose carefully. A thin-walled horn will make a decent knob stick: the tip is cut off at a point where it will fit on to a shank. A threaded rod is inserted into the horn and glued to join it to the shank, and the hollow section is filled with propriety filler, providing additional security to the threaded rod inserted in the horn. A plain or decorated cap is fixed on to the horn, and rounded off and polished.

The procedure for bulking and bending cow horn is similar to dressing sheep horn, but more care and attention is necessary as cow horn will sometimes delaminate (separate) if it is bulked or bent too quickly. Be patient and squeeze the horn a little at a time, and give it sufficient time to cool and set before moving to the next stage.

walls, but they usually have extensive curls that have to be removed so the horn will fit into a press and bulking blocks. A simple tool can be made by an experienced metal worker to grip the horn so the curl can be opened up and straightened sufficiently for it to fit into a bulking press.

A piece of suitably sized steel pipe can be used to straighten the curl if an uncurling tool cannot be obtained, but it is liable to damage the horn.

Uncurling tool.

A pair of cow-horn handles.

Tools and Equipment

Uncurling Tool

Rams' horns are preferred over ewe horns because they are generally larger with thicker

Concave Blocks

Rams' horn often has a deep concave on one side, and this must be removed before attempting to bulk the horn, otherwise a crease will form in the horn during bulking, which will completely ruin the handle. Once a crease has formed it cannot be successfully removed. In order to remove the concave a set of specially made blocks is required to push the convex side of the horn into the concave section, with the aim of making an oval shape. The blocks are used in conjunction with a hydraulic press.

Making Concave Blocks

Hardwood blocks can be made with a few carving chisels and rasps. Cut blocks of hardwood about 5in (125mm) long by 3in (75mm) deep and 3in (75mm) wide. These measurements will vary depending on the size and severity of the curl of the horn.

Place the widest section of the horn on a block, and draw the curved outline shape of the horn on to the block; then make a curved recess (similar to a shallow U shape) into the block to match the curvature of the horn. Repeat this process for each section of the horn until sufficient blocks are made to remove all the concave sections from the horn.

Used carefully the blocks can be utilized several times when made from good quality timber; inferior timber is likely to crack under the pressure of a hydraulic jack. Use blocks with sufficient space at the sides to allow the horn to expand into the space when squeezed in the hydraulic press. Timber blocks can be replaced quite easily if they break or crack in use. However, if it is intended to make a quantity of horn handles it is possible to have a set of aluminium blocks cast in a foundry or by someone experienced in casting aluminium; these blocks are expensive, but will last a lifetime.

Removing the Concave

Removing the concave is a slow process, in which the convex side of the horn is used to push out the concave using the blocks. Heat is applied carefully to the horn using a hot-air gun or gas torch, concentrating most of the heat along the concave side so it becomes softer and weaker than the convex side of the horn. The heated horn is pressed into a block, which effectively turns the horn inside out by forcing the concave out of the horn. The perfect result is when both sides are the same, with the ideal shape being an oval rather like a rugby ball.

Press

A press is essential for dressing all types of horn. It is used to flatten horn after removing the curl and removing a concave, and to align a horn after the shaping procedure. A pair of steel

Concave blocks.

Flattening press.

plates placed between the jaws of a powerful vice can be used to press and align horns, but a better option is to make or obtain a press that is used in conjunction with a hydraulic bottlejack similar to the one shown. This type of press can be used to remove the concave sections and taper the nose, and will flatten the most stubborn horns.

Hydraulic jacks within a range of two to twelve tons are suitable for stickmaking, however when using the higher range ensure that your press and blocks will withstand the pressure of these powerful jacks. Do not attempt to squeeze an unheated (cold) horn in a hydraulic press as it is likely to crack and destroy the horn.

Bulking Blocks

A set of bulking blocks is required to bulk (squeeze) the horn into a solid form before it is shaped around formers to make your chosen style of handle. The minimum set of bulking blocks required is five. The largest block should have a diameter of about 2in (50mm), down to the smallest with a diameter of about 1in (25mm), reducing in sizes by about ¼in (6mm) each.

A more comprehensive set of blocks ranging from 2½in (63mm) down to ¾in (20mm), with reductions of around ⅛in (3mm), is better, as these provide much more control of the bulking sequence and cause less stress and potential damage to the horn. The sharp edges of the blocks must be rounded to prevent them from cutting and tearing into the horn during the bulking process.

Wooden blocks can be used successfully, but they are likely to crack or burn after several times of use; blocks made from aluminium are best, while steel blocks are good but are heavier. Aluminium and steel will withstand the hydraulic pressure and heat better than wooden blocks. All types of block can be made at home using a variety of tools. Sections of aluminium sheeting can be cut using a jigsaw or bandsaw, and bolted together using countersunk set screws. The internal shape is refined using engineering rasps and files designed for use with aluminium. Comprehensive sets of cast aluminium bulking blocks can be purchased from some suppliers (*see* Further Information); the blocks need to be adapted to fit into a bulking press.

Bulking Press

A press is required to hold the bulking blocks in position when they are pressed together using a hydraulic jack, and it must be able to withstand the full hydraulic pressure of the jack. The illustration shows a simple but functional press that is used regularly to bulk horn. A method of holding the top block in position is essential;

Bulking press and block.

the block in the example is held in place using two ¼in (6mm) pins. The lower block sits on a flat plate positioned on top of the jack. The two sides of the press have been lengthened and strengthened to cope with large horns, and they will withstand the hydraulic pressure of a 12 tonne jack.

Neck Press

A neck press is very useful as it enables a straight neck to be formed after the horn has been bulked. A press can be made by cutting a section of steel pipe in two, and welding the two pieces into separate steel channels to give the former sufficient strength. The horn is placed into the former, and the two sections are squeezed together in the hydraulic press, resulting in a straight neck.

If possible try to obtain a neck press that has been accurately machined from steel or aluminium; it is worth the expense if you intend to make several horn handles. The diameter of a neck block should be 1¼in (32mm) or more, which will give sufficient allowance when fitting the handle on to a shank. A larger diameter block of 1⅝in (40mm) is useful when working with large horns. The illustration shows three types of neck press.

Tapered Nose Press

A tapered nose press is used to make a taper shape on the nose of the horn in preparation for turning a nose. It is made from ½in (12mm) steel plate. Cut a length of plate about 5in (125mm) long that will fit inside a 1in (25mm) section of channel; fix it by welding it into position. The

Types of neck press.

Tapered nose press.

thick end of the wedge should be about ½in (12mm), tapering to ⅛in (3mm) over its length. The block is used in a strong vice or hydraulic press, so it must be strong enough to withstand the pressure. A blacksmith or experienced metal worker will make a tapered block easily and at a reasonable cost. (In the image please excuse the terrible welding on my home-made press.)

Nose-Bending Jig

Different styles of nose-bending jig can be made to turn noses on horn. A different style of jig is used to demonstrate turning the nose out on the ram's horn than the one used previously to turn the buffalo horn. This jig is home-made from an offcut of aluminium plate; a length of steel box section is fixed on the under-side, which enables the jig to be held in a vice. A cluster of holes is drilled for a ³⁄₈in- (10mm-)

diameter stainless-steel 'bending bolt'. Another series of holes is drilled around the perimeter of the plate; ½in (12mm) stainless-steel bolts are inserted to anchor the clamp in several differ-ent positions around the jig so the nose can be pulled round the 'bending bolt' from different directions.

This jig provides good control over the horn, but it does require a long sash clamp in order to be successful. The bolts used are stain-less steel as these are stronger than mild steel. In the example illustrated a buffalo horn is used to show how a horn is positioned on the jig.

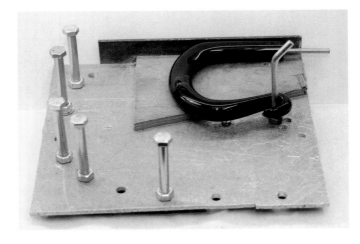

Nose-bending jig.

Making Shepherds' Crooks

The following guide demonstrates how to make the two crooks shown in the image at the beginning of the chapter: these are made from sheep's horn using the equipment described above. Other styles of horn handle can be made using this method with different shaped formers. Making cow-horn handles uses the same technique, although more care and attention will be required when bulking and shaping the horn. Stickmakers have developed a variety of equipment and techniques to bend and shape horn, but essentially they are all based on the principles described in the following sequence.

Step 1: Select a horn: Begin by selecting a horn of sufficient length to make a nose-out crook – 16in (40cm) or more – with substantial walls and a small opening that with care can be bulked.

Step 2: Boil and uncurl the horn: Submerge the horn in boiling water for about twenty-five

minutes. Fasten the hot horn into a strong vice and remove the curl using the uncurling tool. Allow the horn to cool in a straighter position for about five minutes; tie the tool in position until the horn cools. Note that a tapered piece of shank has been inserted into the hollow section of the horn to prevent it from collapsing when it is clamped in a vice during this sequence.

Step 3: Flatten the horn: Before the uncurled horn cools off completely, place it in a flattening press and flatten it; this makes it much easier to fit into the concave or bulking blocks. When the horn has cooled, remove it from the press.

Flattening the uncurled horn.

Uncurling the horn.

Step 4: Begin removing the concave: If a horn needs to have a concave removed, select a suitably sized block for the horn, which will allow it to spread into shape. Use a hot-air gun to heat the first section of the concave. Concentrate the heat on the concave side of the horn, and use the cooler (harder) convex side of the horn to push the heated (softer) concave section of horn into the block. If the horn is hollow, prevent it from collapsing by inserting a piece of tapered shank into the hollow section of the horn. The illustration shows an aluminium block, but a wooden block can also be used

Begin removing the concave.

Step 5: Continue removing the concave: Now that the first section of the concave has been removed, this section is now an oval shape. Note that the horn has followed the shape of the block removing the deep concave. Continue moving along the horn using smaller blocks until all the concave has been removed; continue heating the concave side, and use the convex side to push the horn into the block.

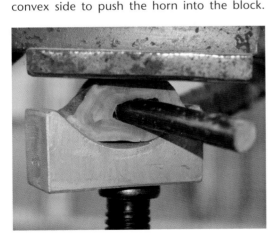

The concave is removed.

When the process is complete, remove any surplus horn, making it into an oval shape before beginning the bulking sequence. Removing the concave will help to prevent creases forming during the bulking process.

Step 6: Bulking the horn: Begin bulking the horn using an appropriate size of block. Avoid using a block that is too big: it is important to control and minimize the movement of the horn in the block – again, note the use of a wooden plug to prevent the horn from collapsing, causing a crease to form. Use a hot-air gun to heat the first section of the horn: apply sufficient heat to soften the horn, but not so much as to burn or scorch the horn; compress the horn on to the wooden plug if fitted.

Drilling out some of the wooden plug allows the diameter of the horn to be reduced under control, and will prevent it from collapsing during the bulking process. It may take several passes to complete the bulking sequence if a large void has to be closed.

Steel drifts can be used instead of wooden plugs for bulking and removing concaves from horn: the tapered drift is withdrawn slowly as the horn is bulked. A range of different sized drifts is required to fit into the various hollow sections of horn. Combinations of wooden and steel drifts can be used.

Starting to bulk the horn.

Step 7: Continue bulking and straighten the neck: Continue bulking along the neck section. Leave a space between the heel position and crown: this will help to form a square heel. Only bulk the first section of the crown at this stage. Next, use a neck block to straighten the curved neck section of the handle. Note that only a small wooden plug is left, which will be removed when a dowel joint is fitted later. *A solid horn is the best option.*

Forming a straight neck.

Step 8: Bulking the crown: Begin bulking the crown. The straightened heel makes

Bulking the crown.

it easier to manipulate the horn in the bulking blocks. Again, select an appropriate sized bulking block that limits the movement in the horn. Heat the horn with a hot-air gun and continue bulking along the crown using smaller blocks as the horn diameter reduces; continue until the nose section is reached. Avoid squeezing the horn too much in one pass as this will mark (or crack) it.

Step 9: Taper the nose: When the crown is bulked, heat the nose of the horn and bulk it with smaller blocks. Follow this by using a tapered nose press to compress the horn, forming a taper on it. This will compress the pith inside the horn and make a good shape when turning the nose out. Allow the horn to cool completely and set in place.

Tapering the nose.

Step 10: Remove the waste from the bulked horn: The bulking process is complete and the nose is tapered ready for turning. Any pieces of unwanted horn that have been formed during the bulking process can be carefully removed with rasps or files.

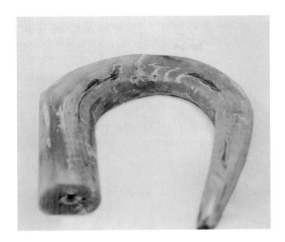

Bulked horn with a tapered nose.

Step 11: Shape the horn: The method of shaping ram's horn uses the same technique and jigs used to shape buffalo horn. Fasten a suitable former on to the jig, and position the horn on to the former; fasten the neck tightly in place so that it will not move during the shaping process. Gently heat the horn, and use clamps to pull the horn on to the former until it fits tightly in position. A piece of flat bar is used to push the tapered nose section on to the former: the flat bar prevents indentations forming in the horn if a clamp is used directly on

Shaping the bulked horn.

this section. At this stage in the shaping process ensure that the nose, crown and heel are all aligned; if necessary use steel wedges under the horn. Allow the horn to cool and set in position before removing it from the jig.

Step 12: Begin turning the nose: (*The nose is turned using the jig featured in the preceding section 'Nose-Bending Jig'.*) Mark the point of the bend on the horn so the outside edge of the turned nose is about ½in (12mm) above the base of the neck, and fasten the horn firmly to a nose-bending jig. Tighten a ³⁄₈in (10mm) bolt in an appropriate hole on to the jig adjacent to the horn, and use a sash clamp to begin the first bend. The sash clamp is secured to one of the ½in (12mm) stainless-steel bolts positioned for pulling the first bend. Gently heat the nose section of the horn, concentrating the heat on the inside of the bend: use a steel rule to direct the heat exactly on to the position of the bend. Do not overheat the horn or it will crack or tear.

Turning the nose.

Step 13: Continue turning the nose: Continue pulling the nose round the bolt; keep changing the position of the clamp so it pulls the horn completely round the bolt. Allow the horn to cool a little between each step so it doesn't revert to its original shape while you are changing the position of the clamp. During the bending maintain gentle heat on the inside of the bend; just maintain sufficient heat to move the horn, so keep checking the tension on the clamp and stop the heat as soon as the horn can be moved.

Continue turning the nose.

Step 14: Complete turning the nose: Complete shaping the nose. The nose can be squeezed very gently in a vice if a tighter turn is required. When the horn has cooled and set in position, remove it from the vice. Carefully remove any waste from the inside of the bend.

Complete the nose.

Step 15: The final shaping: The horn may move slightly during the nose-bending procedure, so take this opportunity to check the shape on the former: make any adjustments as required using gentle heat on the horn, pulling it tightly on to the former using clamps. When the final shaping is complete, leave the horn to cool on the former until it sets in position.

The final shaping of the handle.

Step 16: Dress the horn: Carefully dress the horn using files and abrasives, ensuring that any deep marks are removed. When the horn has reached a satisfactory stage ready for fitting on to a shank, mark the point to drill the hole for the dowel joint.

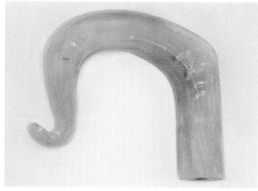

Dressing the horn.

Step 17: Join the handle on to a shank and complete the crook: Use a sharp, flat spade bit to drill out a ⁵/₈in (16mm) hole into the horn. Select a suitable shank that has been straightened, and make a dowel joint to fit into the horn. Glue the joint, and when it has set, complete dressing the horn until it fits perfectly on to the shank. The horn diameter will reduce slightly as it is shaped to match the shank. Fit a ferrule, apply sanding sealer to the shank, and apply a few coats of finish. Complete the handle with a finish of your choice; the one in the illustration has been buffed, polished and waxed.

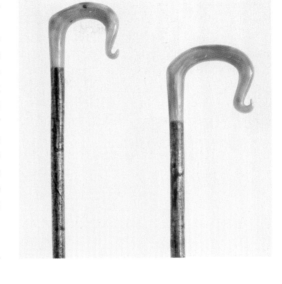

Finished crooks.

DECORATED HANDLES

There is a significant difference between a decorated and a novelty stick: a decorated stick must be functional and fit for its intended purpose, whereas a novelty stick does not have to be practicable – they are generally made for fun and pleasure, and do not have to conform to any of the standards required for a functional stick.

Decorating a stick allows the maker to demonstrate their imagination, artistic flair, talent and skills, but there are some important features that must be complied with when making one of these sticks. The scale, shape and colouring of any feature must be an accurate representation of the subject, the proportions of the decoration must balance with the overall size of the stick, and finally the stick must be serviceable and comfortable to use.

Because a walking or working stick must be functional and fit for purpose, sharp decorations that protrude too much will risk making the handle uncomfortable to hold, so should not be carved on the neck or crown of a handle where the stick is held; they are best positioned on the nose section of the handle. Carvings and decorations are acceptable as long as they are unobtrusive and do not interfere with the use of the stick; sharp points and parts that would be vulnerable to damage should be avoided as much as possible.

Stickmakers use many ingenious methods to include features such as ears, horns and fins in their designs without infringing any of the limitations mentioned above, yet accurately replicating the character of the feature they have carved – for example, in the case of a fish, the fins will be laid flat against the surface of the handle but will have sufficient detail to accurately emulate the fin. Also, the name or initials of the stick's owner may be carved on the sides of the crown or around the neck.

Feathers and scales are good examples of features that can be burnt or scribed into a handle without impeding the functionality of the stick. The snake featured in the illustration below demonstrates how scales and a head can be integrated into a handle without compromising the usefulness of the buffalo-handled crook.

opposite: **Decorated handles.**

Scales burnt on to a handle.

Inspiration and Ideas

Some of the most popular items and characters used regularly to decorate handles and shanks are animals, birds, fish and plants, and the name or initials of the stick's owner. Game birds are frequently depicted, as are birds of prey and small birds such as wrens and kingfishers. Curlews, snipe, ducks and swans make excellent subjects. Salmon and trout are also popular: a leaping trout is an ideal shape for a handle, providing the fins do not make the handle too uncomfortable. Sheep and collie dogs are often carved on to the nose of traditional shepherds' crooks, while thistles, leeks and acorns are used extensively to represent the country of origin of the stick's owner or maker. A huge variety of animals are copied: dogs, horses, badgers, sheep, squirrels, otters, hares and snakes are among the most frequently used. Books with detailed and scaled drawings and sketches of animals, birds and plants can be purchased and are very helpful for beginners.

Pictures and lifelike sketches of all these animals and birds can be found in magazines, books and newspapers and on the internet. Try to take as many photos and pictures as you can, and keep them in an album or file. Digital cameras and mobile phones are ideal for taking your own pictures as they can be carried in a pocket and so are readily available, and most importantly, they take good quality photographs. If you can, try to take several pictures of the subject from various angles to help you make a realistic and accurate carving.

Stickmaking competitions are frequently held throughout the country in conjunction with county agricultural shows and rural fairs and events; the competitions are well worth visiting to see the many different styles of stick on show, and particularly how some of the top makers cleverly integrate their designs

into the sticks. Finally, it is worth considering joining a local stickmaking club or the British Stickmakers Guild, where you can see the different styles and types of stick made by their members, who will generally offer help and advice on their methods of decorating sticks.

Marking Out the Image

Most modern printers have photocopying facilities built into them, that can be accurately scaled up or down so the image suits the size of your handle or shank. When you have an image of suitable size, take some copies, then cut out the shapes of individual features and use these to draw the shape of each one (such as a beak) on to a blank. Use a feature, such as an eye, as datum point for your measurements. A pair of dividers is useful for transferring the key parts of an image accurately on to your handle or shank.

It is helpful to mark the main points of the subject's profile on the blank; for example, you might look for the following: where does the mouth or beak finish in relation to the eyes? Where are the ears positioned in relation to the eyes and mouth? Are the ears swept backwards or forwards from the eyes? Where are the cheeks positioned in relation to the mouth and eyes? Marking some of these features and siting them correctly on the blank in relation to another feature will help to produce a realistic carving.

There is no right or wrong way to carve a figure, but there are proven methods that help the carver to keep on track, such as drawing a centre line along the carving, and always taking measurements from the centre line and another datum point such as the position of the eyes: use these as the main reference points for all the measurements. Replace these marks whenever you remove material, so you maintain the datum point to work with at all times.

Carving the Figure

If the eyes of the subject figure are exactly opposite each other on the side of its head, it is a good idea to a drill a tiny hole through the blank that will become the head, providing it is carefully aligned to ensure that both eye positions are opposite each other. A pillar drill is ideal as it can be set up to drill an accurate hole through the blank.

When carving an object, always ensure that both sides are kept equal and balanced; if the eyes face forwards, ensure they are both level – a lop-sided eye will spoil any carving. Calipers can be used to check that each side of a head and the eyes are positioned equally. Regularly check that the principal feature, such as a nose or beak, is in the centre of the head by maintaining the centre line throughout the carving process. The more points of reference you can use, the more accurate the carving will be; the result should be a carving where all the features are in proportion with each other, giving a balanced and accurate representation of the object you are creating. Attention to detail may take a little longer, but the results will be worthwhile.

Using the main features as datum points, carefully remove unwanted material using some of the tools mentioned in the next section, and the shape of your chosen image will begin to appear. It is the detail that distinguishes a good carving from a mediocre one, so take care to ensure that the features and profiles are accurate. When the eyes of an animal are featured, the colour and fitting must be correct: they will transform the creature and make it look alive and realistic. Other features such as mouth,

ears, nose, nostrils, beak, fur, hair, feathers and cheeks must be represented accurately. When fruit and plants such as thistles and acorns are depicted, it is important that their shape, size and markings are reflected accurately in the carving.

Nature seldom produces square shapes and straight lines, and yet a lot of carvings of natural items are made using these shapes and lines, which spoils both the effect and the look of the carving. These details are difficult to achieve unless you have a natural artistic flair; however, copying accurately from a model, photo or image will often produce a reasonable handle for a stick. Be patient and take care when carving, work to the marks you have made marking out, and avoid cutting off too much material at once; check the carving constantly, using the copied images and cutouts as guides throughout the carving process.

Tools and Equipment

There are tools of many different types and quality available to shape and carve the range of materials used in stickmaking, so choose carefully; always try to obtain well made, good quality tools as there are plenty of inferior ones available. Tools for carving and shaping need to be kept sharp, and must maintain their edge during use; poor quality tools soon lose their edge, making carving more difficult and far less enjoyable.

Carving Chisels and Knives

A lot of work on timber and sheep horn can be successfully carried out using traditional carving chisels, rasps and files. There are four basic types of carving chisel used to carve

Carving chisels.

Rifflers and detail rasps.

Riffler Rasps

Riffler rasps are used for detailed shaping, and will reach into difficult places on the carving; they are generally sold in sets. Rasps especially made for work on timber are useful for shaping, and are particularly good for making wooden handles.

Needle files, modelling knives and micro planes can be used for miniature and detailed carvings; an illuminated magnifying glass is very useful for fine, intricate work.

Power Carving Tools

Power carvers and multi-tools are ideal for carving and shaping antler and buffalo horn when used with rotary burrs to remove material. Hand-held and flexible-drive units with numerous attachments are available for these machines; some reciprocating carving heads with chisels operate with the more powerful units, and can be used on timbers and ram's horn.

Small, powered units used for fine work such as model making, jewellery and glasswork are now popular with stickmakers who are making handles with very detailed and life-like carvings. These variable speed control units are connected by a light cable to a small tool holder and operate at speeds often exceeding 30,000rpm, and require suitable accessories that don't burn at these speeds. They are very effective for detailing fur, feathers and other features in most materials, and they work well in antler and horn.

timber, which can also be used to carve ram's horn: these are straight, skew, gouge and V chisels. They are available in different sizes and sweeps, and can be obtained in sets or individually.

Carving knives are very useful, and are also available with several different shaped blades.

Pocket whittling knives with several blades are popular as they can be carried easily anywhere the carver goes. Carving knives always work best when kept sharp: sharpening stones, strops and wheels all work well with knives and chisels.

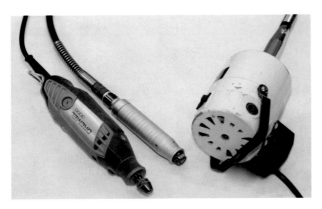

Rotary power tools.

Pyrography

Pyrography is the term used for burning images on to the carving material, and is a process that can be used on most of the materials used in stickmaking to form details such as fur, feathers, hair, scales and wrinkles. Horn can be burnt with care, but it emits a terrible smell so avoid using it indoors. Some materials such as plastics, acrylic and resin do not burn successfully, so always practise on a test piece first.

There are two basic types of pyrography machine, and both use electricity to heat the tips and nibs; the first type uses solid tips, is similar to a soldering iron, and usually operates directly off mains voltage. The tips are of solid brass and range from flat points through to sharp ones; they can be inserted into the handle, which heats them to a high temperature when switched on. The disadvantage of this system is that the temperature is fixed and cannot be varied – all the burning is carried out at the same temperature – which causes the handle to get very hot.

The second and most popular type uses wire elements (nibs) that are fitted on to a pen, which is connected to a control unit that varies the temperature of the nib. The pen operates at a low voltage, making it a safe tool to handle in workshop conditions. Wire elements of different thickness can be used with these machines to form thick or thin lines. The wire can be easily bent and shaped with a small pair of round-nosed pliers; it can also be flattened when the wire is heated up to a red heat to form a sharp blade for making very fine lines. Specialized nibs can be obtained either individually or in sets for specific types of work such as bird carving, and some are interchangeable with other manufacturers' equipment. The variable temperature settings are extremely useful, as infinite control can be achieved of the element temperature, which is essential for some materials. Using different temperature settings and nibs, a range of colouring can be achieved on a single piece of material, allowing different aspects of a figure to be highlighted.

Colouring

Colours can be used to embellish and enhance carvings and etchings on walking and working

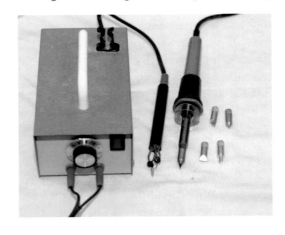

Pyrography units.

sticks. There are numerous types of substance that can be used to colour sticks, such as paint, stain, ink, dye, varnish and burning.

Stain should be used on untreated wood as it works best when it is allowed to soak into the fibres of the timber; one problem is that the stain can travel along the grain, making it difficult to obtain sharp lines. Black stain can be used with some success to conceal cracks and flaws in buffalo horn.

Dyes and inks are similar to stain and are best used on untreated surfaces; they are liable to run when used with fibrous materials.

Paints are best for detailed colouring, and there is a wide range to choose from. Model paints are popular, as are acrylics, as these can be obtained in small quantities, making them ideal for stickmakers who only use small amounts at a time. It is important to know the make-up of all paints used so that a compatible finish can be applied to protect it; some paints and finishes react adversely with each other.

Some varnishes are coloured and can be used to enhance the overall colouring of natural barks and timbers; they are not intended to be used for detailed colouring work.

Iridescent paints are used to colour bird feathers such as pheasants, starlings, ducks and kingfishers, and are very realistic when applied correctly.

Finally, when applying colouring, attempt to replicate accurately the natural colour of the animal, bird or plant you are copying. If you intend to enter competitions with your sticks it is imperative that the correct colours are used when decorating them – too often people spoil their carvings by using incorrect colouring, and their sticks are put to the back of the stand. However, it has become acceptable to use pyrography as a method of shading a carving, so colouring with paints is not essential – although when the correct colours are used and a perfect likeness is achieved, it could be a winner.

Two Carved Heads

The following step-by-step guides demonstrate how to carve heads on timber and buffalo horn using some of the tools and techniques described earlier. Being a member of a stick-making club is an advantage – both the heads featured in the following guides were made with guidance from two experienced craftsmen who attended club meetings and gave advice on the methods and techniques they used to shape heads. The two heads featured are the author's version of making the handles under guidance; other club members made similar but not identical heads, which shows how individual perceptions of one item can vary. Timber and horn were used as this demonstrated the different tools needed to shape the two different materials: carving chisels and knives work well with wood, whereas rotary tools work best with buffalo horn.

Making a Duck Head

The carved head featured is based on a decoy duck head; it has been reduced in size to make it suitable for a stick handle. Tim Morgan makes decoy ducks, and over a few lessons helped club members to make duck heads. The technique described can be applied to most types of carving, irrespective of the material used.

Step 1: Obtain pictures or drawings of the type of image you wish to carve. Make some suitably sized scaled copies that can be cut into templates to draw round, or which can be glued on to a blank.

Step 2: Using the templates, mark the outline of the duck on to a flat block, ensuring the main features such as eyes are accurately positioned on the blank using a soft pencil. Alternatively use carbon paper to transfer the main features of a picture on to the blank.

Step 3: Cut out the shape of the duck, leaving a little spare material in case of a mistake. Mark a centre line around the shape: this is the first datum point for all measurements. Next mark the position of the eyes, because duck's eyes are exactly opposite each other: a ¹/₈in (3mm) hole can be drilled from one side of the blank to the other. Ensure the blank is perpendicular before drilling through it. The two eye positions and the centre line can all be used as datum points for all measurements. Calipers can be used to measure distances from the datum points.

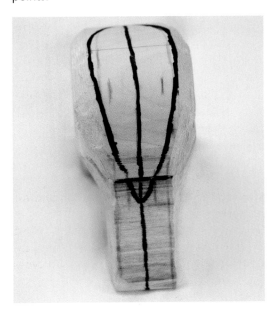

Roughly cut duck head.

Step 4: Begin removing waste material, ensuring the centre line is replaced as soon as possible after cutting off any waste. Carving chisels, knives, rasps and rifflers were used to remove waste wood. Identify the widest point of the head and mark each side of the blank with a

large prominent dot: these two high points must not be carved or removed until the head is finished. Ensure that the width of each side of the head is the same distance from the centre line: check this with calipers.

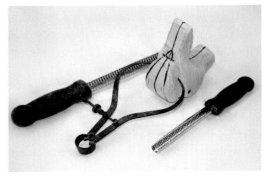

The high points are marked.

Step 5: Mark a point to drill a ⁵/₁₆in (8mm) hole in the base of the neck for a stud joint; drill out the hole and glue a section of threaded studding into the handle. Ensure the base of the handle has a flat surface before gluing in the studding so a close-fitting joint is achieved. When the glue sets the handle can be held by the studding to complete shaping the handle. Note that the centre line remains in place for use as a datum point for all future measurements.

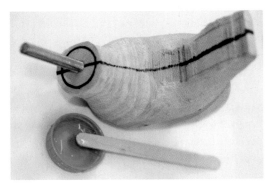

The studding is glued into the handle.

Step 6: Note the way the duck's beak fits on to the head. The beak is parallel and does not come to a point (a common mistake), and it is arched near the head. Using the eyes, measure exactly where the beak joins on to each side of the head; use the centre line to mark the central section of the beak-to-head joint. A duck always appears to be smiling, so it is important that this feature is replicated when cutting the upper and lower sections of the beak.

Continue shaping the head until it can be fixed on to a shank, making sure the head and shank are perfectly aligned and that a smooth transition between the two parts can be achieved. Glue the head on to the shank, and when the adhesive has set, complete the head so it is ready for the final details to be added.

The head is fitted on to the shank.

Step 7: Complete shaping the head and blend the joint so there is a smooth transition between the head and shank. The head can now be decorated. The details can be added using carving chisels and knives, rotary burrs and cutters or pyrography. Glass eyes will be used in the example: the small holes will be

enlarged to make eye sockets to suit the glass eyes.

In the example it was decided to texture the head using a pyrography tool and nibs. To get the best results with pyrography, a smooth surface is required, as a nib is difficult to control on a rough surface. The head was smoothed using 180g abrasive.

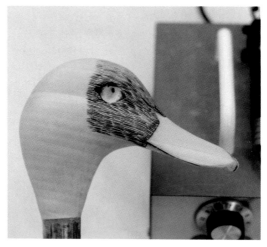

Beginning to texture the head.

Step 8: The texturing is progressing and the eye sockets have been enlarged.

The texturing progresses.

Step 9: The texturing is complete: the size of the feathers has increased closer to the base of the neck, and the eye sockets have been darkened using the pyrography nib to burn the surface of the wood.

Texturing is complete.

Step 10: The glass eyes are fitted and the joint is finished. The texturing has been shaded using pyrography nibs set at various temperatures. Colouring the head was considered but it was decided to use the natural colour of the wood and the shading to produce the finished handle.

The handle is sealed using cellulose sanding sealer, and is finished with a matt lacquer.

The finished stick.

Making a Hare Handle from Buffalo Horn

Step 1: The hare handle is made from a pre-shaped buffalo horn knob handle available from some of the suppliers listed (*see* Further Information]. We all need help, and this design and technique was learnt from Martin Wilde who is very experienced in carving intricate heads on antler and horn. Rotary burrs, files and abrasives were used to shape the handle. The first stages of the carving are similar to the previous example; begin by sketching the main profile of the hare's head on to the blank to determine if the scale and size of the figure will fit on to the pre-shaped blank.

A pre-shaped knob handle.

Step 2: Draw a centre line around the blank; then measure and mark the main profile points of the hare's head on to the pre-shaped horn. It is important at this early stage to ensure that all the features are drawn to scale to make certain that they are balanced and can be used as datum points for the carving. Mark the cheeks of the hare as they are the widest point. Use the eyes and the centre line as the main datum points, and take all measurements, such as the position of the ears and nose, from the eyes. Using these measurements, carefully begin to cut out the main features of the profile.

Step 3: Use rotary tools to cut out the shapes in the horn. Start by marking the eye positions, and then the low and high points on the horn so the profile of the head can be cut on to the block of horn. Examples are the position of the forehead in relation to the eyes, or perhaps the start and finish points of the ears. Take care when using rotary tools as they can remove material very quickly, and a mistake can be difficult to rectify. Begin to shape the contours of the head, ears and nose. Do not reduce the widest point of the cheeks.

The head is shaped and polished.

Start shaping the head.

Step 4: Continue shaping the head using fine rotary tools and needle files. Enlarge the eye sockets, and glue a pair of brown glass eyes into the head. Continue dressing the head and remove any deep marks and scratches from the horn using fine abrasives. When all the deep marks have been removed, buff and polish the horn. Polishing at this stage will highlight any scratches or marks which can be removed.

Step 5: A tapered nickle collar will be fitted to add some character to the stick. Obtain a suitably sized collar for the handle, and cut a recessed dowel on to the horn so the collar fits smoothly on the horn.

The dowel is cut to fit the collar.

Step 6: A dowel is cut on to a straightened shank to fit into the smaller end of the tapered collar to give a smooth transition over the complete joint and collar. The handle is glued on to the shank.

The handle is joined to the shank.

Step 7: When the glue has set, begin texturing the head using a fine pyrography nib. It is important to carry out the texturing on a very smooth surface otherwise it is difficult to control the movement of the nib. It is worth practising the burning technique on a waste piece of horn to learn the best tem-

Begin texturing the head.

perature to set the machine at, and also to learn how much speed and pressure is required to create the textured fur. Start near the nose and work towards the neck so the textured fur flows in the same direction of the growing fur.

Step 8: Continue carefully adding the textured fur on to the head. It may take several hours to complete, depending on your experience. Shading can be achieved by altering the nib temperature and the speed at which the nib is moved on the horn. It may be necessary to add more texturing once the head is brushed with a fine wire brush.

The texturing is complete.

Step 9: Complete the texturing and remove any debris from the handle using a fine brass or a stiff bristle brush. The horn, eyes and collar can be gently polished using a rotary polishing mop.

Cut the shank to length and fit a ferrule, seal the shank and finish with a product of your choice. A matt finish can be applied to the handle.

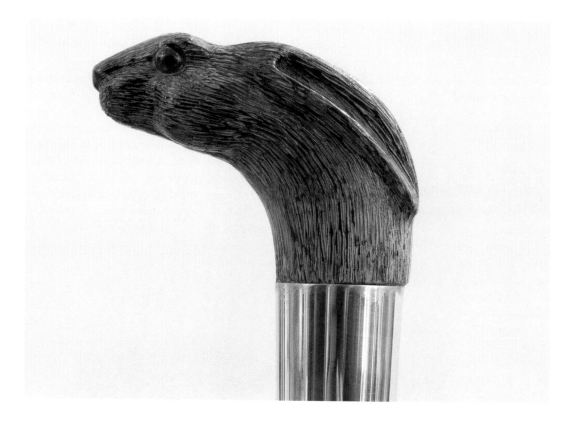

The finished head.

When the decoration is complete and has dried, cut the shank to length, smooth off the bark and fit a ferrule. Apply a suitable finish to the head and shank; several coats may be required to obtain a perfect result.

In Summary

These methods can be adapted for making carved objects and decorations on any stick.

The important aspects to remember are these:

- Use one or more features as a datum point
- Keep a centre line in place throughout the carving
- Start and finish with the widest point of the subject
- Take regular measurements from a datum point, and only remove the bits that are not required

FURTHER INFORMATION

Suppliers and Organizations

Axminster Tools and Machinery
The Trafalgar Way, Axminster, Devon EX13 SSN
Tel. 01297 302370
Web www.axminster.co.uk.
Supplier of machinery, power and hand tools

Robert R. Wilkinson
Callicrafts, Wellhaven, Bridge of Cally, Blairgowrie, Perthshire PH10 7JL
Tel. 01250 886339 (evenings)
Supplier of deer antler

Dafydd Davies
Fron-Villa, Llanddewi, Brefi, Nr Ceredigion, Mid Wales SY25 6RS
Tel. 01974 298566 (evenings)
Email dafyddsticks@btinternet.com
Stickmaker and supplier of stickmaking components

STS (North Wales) Ltd
Llanrwst, Conway LL26 0HU
Tel. 01492 640664
www.glasseyes.com
Supplier of a large range of glass eyes suitable for stickmaking

Peter Child
The Old Hyde, Little Yeldham, Nr Halstead, Essex CO9 4QT
Tel. 01787 237291
www.peterchild.co.uk
Supplier of pyrography machines and turning tools

The British Stickmakers Guild (BSG)
www.thebsg.org.uk
The principal stickmaking organization in the UK. It has around 2,000 members from around the world. It publishes four magazines a year and organizes several stickmaking shows around the UK. Provides links to other stickmaking groups

Martin Hyslop Director
The Highland Horn Company Ltd
Tough na Corach, Knockmuir, Brea, Avoch, Easter Ross IV9 8RD
Tel. 01381 622488
www.highlandhorn@btinternet.com
Supplier of raw materials to stickmakers

Keith Pickering
The Stickman, The Walled Garden, Cleveland Way, Helmsley, York YO62 5AH
Tel. 01439 771450
www.thestickman.co.uk
Stickmaker and supplier of a wide range of stickmaking materials

Tim Dunning
The End House, Burton Lane, East Coker, Yeovil, Somerset BA22 9LJ
Tel. 07585706415
Email timdunning2013@btinternet.com
Supplier of a wide range of shanks including knob and block sticks; timber also available

Charlie Walker
Walkers sticks,
www.walkers-sticks
email Cwalkerssticks@aol.com
Stickmaker and author of Traditional Stickmaking

Woodworks Craft Suppliers, PO Box 102, Caldcot NP26 9AG
Tel. 01633 400847
Web www.woodworkscraftsupplies.co.uk
Suppliers of pyrography and carving machines

INDEX

OTHER TITLES FROM CROWOOD

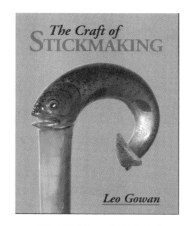

ISBN 978 1 86126 375 9

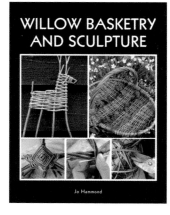

ISBN 978 1 84797 681 9

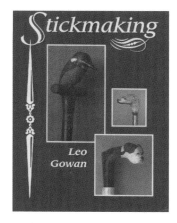

ISBN 978 1 86126 098 7

ISBN 978 1 78500 021 8

ISBN 978 1 84797 770 0

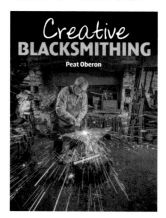

ISBN 978 1 78500 033 1

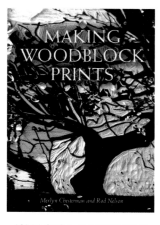

ISBN 978 1 84797 903 2

ISBN 978 1 84797 744 1

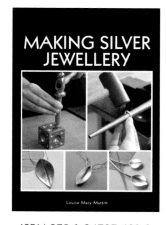

ISBN 978 1 84797 683 3